A Study of
the Pseudo-Map Cycle of Arthurian Romance

A Study of
the Pseudo-Map Cycle of
Arthurian Romance

TO INVESTIGATE ITS HISTORICO-GEOGRAPHIC
BACKGROUND AND TO PROVIDE
A HYPOTHESIS AS TO ITS FABRICATION

by

J. Neale Carman

THE UNIVERSITY PRESS OF KANSAS
Lawrence/Manhattan/Wichita

Preface

The study that follows originated with the sole intention of investigating the geography of the *Mort Artu* and of the beginning of the Prose *Lancelot*. Progress in that fruitful task also revealed probable historical background, which turned out to be of such extensive and varied nature as to give rise to an hypothesis concerning the manner of fabrication of the Cycle. The hypothesis necessarily takes into account the ideologies exhibited in the pseudo-Map Cycle. It is my hope that the readers of this study will discern material valuable, not only in recognizing when, where, and how the Cycle was written, but also in measuring aesthetic and intellectual qualities of the Cycle.

After the manuscript of this study had reached tentative completion, it received serious and detailed criticism from three co-workers in the field of Arthurian romance. To them I gratefully tender my thanks, and to them the study owes great improvement both in form and in the presentation of the facts and arguments. They are Professors Norris J. Lacy and Myra Olstead Hinman of the University of Kansas and Professor William Roach of the University of Pennsylvania. From Professor Roach also came encouragement to develop the last chapter when, without knowledge of the preceding chapters, he saw a preliminary sketch of it. I do not claim that either he or the other two agree with speculative conclusions, but their sympathetic reception of the ideas that I have proposed leads me to hope that the study will not lack interest for other readers.

Contents

1 ❦ Continental Geography— Benoic and Gaunes

he geography of Arthurian romances is usually fanciful, but in the pseudo-Map Cycle or Vulgate Cycle, the Lancelot-Grail Corpus, we sometimes find mention of places in terms sufficiently precise to warrant investigation based upon these topographical data. Examples justifying this assertion appear in paragraphs soon to follow. When the locations of episodes are known, historical reminiscences within them become more evident. Scholars have used allusions to places in the *Lais* of Marie de France as evidence that certain personages whom she mentions lived within the domains of Henry II; in other words, they have identified the "cunte Willame" of her *Ysopet* with an English earl. In the case of the pseudo-Map Cycle, once we are convinced through supporting geographical evidence that it contains passages inspired by contemporary history, more of them become perceptible without such bolstering. Thus the episodes of *False Guenevere* in the Prose *Lancelot* and of False Baldwin in thirteenth-century Flanders seem related. Knowledge of places and events with which an author seems familiar may render his work both more intelligible and more significant. Charles d'Orléans's ballade, "En regardant vers le pays de France," would mean less if we did not know that he was a prisoner in England. Such background is therefore worth study in itself. In the pseudo-Map Cycle the spectacle of King Ban looking back toward burning Trebes, when the reader perceives a historic parallel, may awaken a greater response in him.

The geographical and historical evidence in the pseudo-Map Cycle, once unveiled, seems to imply that there are several authors acquainted with different settings and interested in different events somewhat scattered in time and space. The most salient contrasts in their ideology within the Cycle have already been the subject of much discussion

1

among scholars. Light from the history and geography that the Old French authors expected their readers to know sometimes better illuminates their moral and intellectual convictions. Furthermore, it provides the glow that has allowed me to grope on toward a hypothesis as to how these writers happened to be united in the production of a single work, at once so loosely and so complexly organized. The evidence for it is something more than deductions built upon deductions. Additional history can be invoked in support, also data not properly history. The Grail passage in Helinand's chronicle, viewed from a new angle, becomes a bit of a prop.

The names Benoic and Gaunes, "noms fictifs," F. Lot says (LEt 147),[1] recur repeatedly in the pseudo-Map Cycle. In the *Mort Artu* they are the names of cities (Benoic appears in 127.2; and Gaunes in 130.52 et passim) and also of kingdoms (125.9–10; 56.22, etc.). Lancelot, banished from Logres (England), reaches Benoic, his "terre" (124.15), after having stopped for the night on his journey from the port of debarkation. He had sailed apparently from the mouth of the Humber, and therefore would have landed at Boulogne, Calais, or more likely, Wissant. His first travel on land is consequently in the Flamingo-Picard region. For the *Mort Artu* Benoic could thus very well have been situated where Normandy is. When Arthur arrives to make war upon Lancelot, he follows the same path, but finding all castles in Benoic well defended, he attacks none. At Gawain's insistence he marches on to besiege the city of Gaunes "ou li rois Boorz et li rois Lioniax et Lancelos et Hestor demeurent atout leur pooir" (130.37–39). Nothing is said about the direction or distances, but we have learned that Gaunes is farther from Logres than Benoic.

After the duel won by Lancelot from Gawain, King Arthur commands that the camp before Gaunes be struck, for he "ira en Gaule sejourner" (159.29) to care for his sorely wounded nephew. Accordingly he installs himself in "une cité que l'en apele Meaus" (160.1–2). Thus the Champenoise town of Meaux is in "Gaule" and not in the kingdom of Gaunes. We must conclude that it is a border town, because Arthur would not transport a man wounded as severely as

---

[1] See the Bibliography for the system of reference by sigla. Parenthetic references beginning with a Roman numeral are to the volume, page, and line numbers in H. Oskar Sommer's edition of *The Vulgate Version of the Arthurian Romances*; references beginning with an Arabic numeral are to the section and line numbers in Jean Frappier's 1954 edition of *La Mort le roi Artu*.

Gawain farther than necessary. The *Mort Artu* repeatedly gives evidence that its author understands the debilitating effect of bad wounds. For the author of the *Mort Artu* the kingdom of Gaunes, which one reaches by traversing Benoic-Normandy and which one quits by a short journey from the city of Gaunes to Meaux, seems to represent the Ile de France, and the city of Gaunes is Paris, its capital. To both F. Lot and J. Frappier, Meaux seemed to be chosen as the spot for Gawain's recovery for no reason other than the predilection of the author, in whom they are therefore inclined to see a man born in Champagne. There is no need to reject their conjecture, but the explanation just advanced does away with the need of finding any other than a topographical reason for naming Meaux.

In the *Agravain* section of the Prose *Lancelot* (Volume V of Sommer's edition), King Claudas, usurper in Gaunes, and his ill-gotten Kingdom occupy fifty-nine pages (V.319–77), with a separate introductory section of eight more (256–63). Arthur and his knights war against Claudas who, when they invade, makes the city of Gaunes his headquarters. The author of the *Agravain* names Benoic, town and kingdom, but no important action takes place there. The first forces from Great Britain are led by Gawain, Bohort, and Lionel. When they land on the Continent, they do so in Flanders: "lendemain se mistrent parmi flandres qui lors ert apelee flanmesgues" (V.337.2). They defeat the Flemish count and lay waste his territory. From it they pass into Gaul, where there is no resistance. That land at the moment is without a king, the last king having died during a trip to Rome. Gaul is left unscathed. Next the army reaches the kingdom of Claudas (V.338.16).

The realm is unnamed, but we soon learn that the chief city is Gaunes. There is a preliminary battle near the castle of "Pinegon" (V.338), but most of the action takes place near or before Gaunes or at the castle of the "Cor," which is not far away, for men can be brought out to it from the city in a few hours. With the arrival of Roman forces to aid Claudas, Gawain and his friends feel the need of reinforcements for themselves, and King Arthur and Lancelot receive an appeal. Under their leadership a new army departs from Logres. After landing, apparently in Flanders, though this time the county is not named, it marches to join the other British forces before Gaunes (V.370 ff.). As it passes through Gaul, the army bivouacs at the castle of Bestoc (V.371.20), a stop marked by the celebrated victory of King Arthur over Frolle, Comte d'Allemagne, in single combat. Thus, the later forces from Britain have apparently followed a route similar to that of their predecessors, though there are still fewer specifications as to the details of the itinerary. The account of battles before Gaunes contributes no information to us about locations. After the Romans are defeated, Claudas flees from the kingdom of Gaunes; its people then welcome their rightful lords, Bohort and Lionel. The names Pinegon (variant, Pagon) and Bestoc resemble nothing in the gazetteer of France closely enough to suggest possibilities of identification. The geography of the *Agravain* seems similar but not identical to that of the *Mort Artu*. Gaul seems to occupy the same area as neglected Benoic. Claudas's usurped kingdom might be the Ile de France or a kingdom in the Loire valley or somewhere else. The topographical notions are so vague that even naming Flanders seems remarkable.

Pierre Gallais, in his article on Bleheri published in the *Actes du VIIe Congrès national de littérature comparée*, says "Pour les auteurs du grand cycle en prose le Poitou, ou plus exactment La Rochelle en Poitou sera la base de débarquement des armées bretonnes, d'où elles se rendront soit en Touraine (Gaunes), soit en Armorique (Broceliande)" (Ga 53). In a note he supports his affirmation by references to Sommer's volumes II and VII. His first reference is to II.110, note 3, which presents a passage not in Sommer's base manuscript but found in MSS. numbers 105 and 9123. Merlin has gathered a force in Benoic and Gaunes, and the variant passage says that he and his levy journey till they "vindrent en la rochele en poitau" where they find shipping. Nothing is said about the direction or length of the journey. Another passage (II.256) makes Arthur, Ban, and Bohort the Elder take ship at Dover and sail to La Rochelle. Thence with a march apparently extending over parts of two days, they reach the Loire (II.260) and are in the realm of Benoic. Still another passage (II.281) makes Gawain, as he returns from ravaging Claudas's lands, stop first at Benoic and then ride on to Gaunes and thence to La Rochelle. The last of the passages (II.376) has Merlin direct that armies from Benoic and Gaunes shall sail from La Rochelle for Great Britain. The armies gather at Gaunes, and go then to La Rochelle.

The reference made by M. Gallais to Volume VII, *Le Livre d'Artus*, show that its author had similar locations in mind. Leaving La Rochelle, his characters reach Gaunes first, Benoic later (VII.160; 139.12). There is no doubt that in these passages we are in the valley of the Loire and in the country to the south of it, but M. Gallais's assignment of the Gaunes of Sommer's Volume II to Touraine may be questioned. Benoic is on the Loire and Gaunes is between it and La

Rochelle, easy of access. Gaunes must be Poitou or Anjou; and Benoic, Anjou or Touraine.

All other authors of the pseudo-Map Cycle must have become acquainted with the names Benoic and Gaunes through the account appearing at the beginning of the Prose *Lancelot* proper, where the evidence as to the location of Benoic and Gaunes is much more copious.

In the first 118 pages of Sommer's Volume III of his Vulgate Cycle, the pseudo-Map Cycle, Lancelot's career is traced from infancy till the moment when his knightly career is to begin. It recounts many other events; these are centered about King Claudas. Except for two short episodes concerning visits to Arthur's court, the action takes place in the kingdoms of Benoic and Gaunes. The 118 pages may well be called the Book of Benoic and Gaunes and will hereafter be referred to as the *Benoic-Gaunes*.

It begins: "En la marche de gaule & de la petite bertaigne auoit . ij. Rois anchienement" (III.3.1–2); they were "bans de benoich" and "bohours de gannes." The romance thus presents us with both fictional and factual toponyms. Ban of Benoic had a neighbor "qui marchisoit a lui deuers berri . qui lors estoit apelee la terre deserte . li siens voisin auoit non claudas . si estoit sires de bohorges . & del pais tout enuiron" (III.3.12–14).

The explanation of "terre deserte" is a case in which the author of the *Benoic-Gaunes* identifies his fictional name by means of an actual toponym; such cases are rare, but by them the reader is warned that the romance may use fictional inventions or adaptations to replace real geographic terminology. Often, without explanation, the author resorts to disguises, sometimes slight, sometimes more radical. Claudas's uncle Patrice is specified as being by "anchiserie" lord of Charrot and Duns (III.28.28). The name Duns, the author informs us, had later been lengthened to Essorduns, according to Sommer's edition (III.28:31), but variants in several manuscripts give Ysoudun or Yssoudun.[2]

---

[2] BN 118 Ysoudun, 344 Yssoudun(s) as presented below, BM Royal 19.C.13 Ysoduns, Bod. Rawlinson Qb6 Ysouduns. The general manuscript tradition of the pseudo-Map Cycle says, like Sommer's edition, that Patrice's son changed the name of Dun to Issoudun, but in certain other respects the passage offers difficulties in all the manuscripts that I have consulted. Sommer's version from BM Additional 10293 is: "auoit non patriches . & estoit sires dun castel dales gannes deuers solel escousant que claudas li auoit doune . Mais par anchiserie estoit sires dun chastel qui ot non charrot . & vn autre dales qui ot non duns . mais au tans essent li fil chelui patriche qui trop fu preus & uigueres & fu apeles esordes pour che que trop estoit petis ses nons . Com a

Charost and Issoudun to the southwest of Bourges must be meant. Lot further identifies Saint Cirre (III.76.36) with Sancerre (LEt 149*n*4); he offers no evidence from the romance to support his assertion. Probably he is right, though there are many places called Saint Cyr, some in the region. We shall see other examples in the *Benoic-Gaunes* where the author applies the name of an obscure place to another of more note. The lords of Dun and Saint Cirre were chosen to aid in protecting Claudas from the wrathful people of Gaunes. It seems logical that for this purpose hereditary vassals of Claudas from "la terre deserte" (Berry) should be chosen rather than nobles bred in the usurped kingdom of Gaunes. The manner in which these proper names are presented gives rise to the expectation that the author would apply elsewhere similar techniques, sometimes changing a letter or two, sometimes making greater alterations, but generally allowing those familiar with an area to recognize the place designated, either because its real name is barely disguised or because the place has been assigned a slightly altered toponym occurring in the area. In the case of the change from Dun to Issoudun he warns his readers; he lets them guess in the case of Charost and Sancerre.

The *Benoic-Gaunes* says Claudas's ancestral realm was Berry; it was in twelfth-century Capetian territory; the lands to the west were held until 1204 by the Plantagenets. Claudas's hostility to domination from the west is expressed in the following passage: "Aramons [Lord of Brittany] auoit desous lui Gaunes [Sommer's text and BN 751 and

---

si boin chastel & si plentiueus . si fu autant a dire essorduns comme li dus essout" (III.28.26–32).

MS BN 344 offers a better reading except for the name corresponding to Charost: "[Patrides] estoit sires d'un chastel de lez Gaunes devers souleil couchant que Claudas li avoit doné. Mais par ançoiserie estoit sires del chastel de Sarroc et d'un autre chastel de lez Sarroc qui estoit apelez au tens de lors Duns, mais el tens le filz celui Patride qui tant fu preus fu apelez Yssoudun por ce que trop petit estoit ses nons com a si bon chastel et si plenteureus. Et ce fu a dire Yssouduns come dons Isont" (fol. 189d). The only difficulty that I see in this version is in the last word. There is no doubt that the next to the last letter is an "n" because it is represented by a tilde, but the scribe must have misread "Isout." I take this sentence to have meant as first written that the name Dun was too small for such a splendid castle, that therefore it should be called after Isolt the Blond. Thus we have here testimony to the popularity of the *Tristan*. The author of the romance was apparently aware of the meaning of Celtic "dun," fortified place, as exemplified in Verdun and Issoudun and a close neighbor of the latter, Dun-sur-Auron (whence Dunois), but the scribe of 344 apparently thought that it was a question of a gift, and so wrote "dons."

Despite garblings, all readings exhibit the point of the author's technique that I wish to demonstrate—his adaptation of real names for his romance.

768 read "gaule," but BN 754, 118, and 344, BM Royal 19.C.13, and Oxford Rawlinson Qb6 have "Gaunes," which must be correct] . et benoich & toute la terre iusque a la marche dauuergne & de gascoigne . & deuoit auoir desous lui le regne de boorges Mais claudas ne li counisoit mie . ne seruice ne li uoloit rendre . ains auoit fait signour del roi de gaule" (III.3.19–22). Aramont's holdings outside of Britanny are those which in the twelfth century belonged to the Plantagenets. With them are contrasted Capetian lands.

If the kingdoms of Benoic and Gaunes, ruled by brothers, are on the march of Brittany, and Benoic borders Berry, they necessarily occupy Anjou-Touraine, a unit subject in the twelfth century to the counts of Anjou, and Poitou, which fell to them by marriage in 1152. Benoic, capital of the kingdom of the same name, is on the Loire, for a judicial duel takes place "en la praerie de benoych entre loirre et arsie" (III.12.15). The realm of Benoic is thus located on the older Angevin territory, and Gaunes must occupy the site of Poitou, for, we shall see, it is not on the Loire. Further investigation shows that for the scene of events taking place in Benoic and Gaunes the author had in mind a more restricted territory between, but not including, Angers and Poitiers.

A great deal of action takes place in the City of Gaunes. It possesses a gate which "deuers bertaigne estoit" (III.91.33). It is therefore not far from Brittany. It is some seven leagues from a castle which "seoit sor la riuiere de loire" (III.74.36). This fixes the distance inland. In Poitou these data describe the location of the town of Thouars, concerning which a quotation from Boussard is appropriate:

> Quant au vicomte de Thouars, c'était sans contredit le plus puissant vassal du comte de Poitiers. . . . La vicomté s'étendait en bordure de l'Anjou et du comté de Nantes. . . . elle commandait ainsi toutes les voies de communication entre le Poitou, l'Anjou et la Bretagne: c'est vraiment une seigneurie des marches, avec tout ce que cette situation comporte d'avantageux pour le seigneur. . . . Le vicomte de Thouars menait un train princier et possédait une maison, comprenant, comme celle des rois et des grands féodaux, un sénéchal, un pannetier, un chambrier . . . . (BoH 115–16)

Gaunes, of similar importance and accurately located, must be regarded as on the emplacement of Thouars.

Taking into account the habits of name alteration of the author of the *Benoic-Gaunes*, the name Gaunes can be related, within the area, to Gennes on the Loire and Monts-sur-Guesnes inland. Both are some twenty miles from Thouars, with Gennes to the north and Monts-sur-Guesnes to the east.[3] This onomastic case shows the transfer of a somewhat deformed toponym from a place of small significance to a spot of more importance not too far away.

The castle seven leagues from Gaunes located on the Loire belonged to Graier, a cousin of Ban. Here is the passage identifying him according to MS. Bibliothique Nationale 118: "[Graier] estoit sires d'un moult riche chastel qui estoit a moins de . vii . lieues d'illeuc [Gaunes] pres de Benoyc; ce chasteau avoit a non Haut Mur et seoit sur la riviere de Loire moult en haut par devers le tertre." The reading in Sommer's edition (III.74.34–37) differs in an essential respect; instead of the last four words, it runs, "par deuers la terre deserte." MSS. BN 339, 344, and 754, and Oxford Rawlinson Qb6, have eight leagues instead of seven, but otherwise agree with Sommer. British Museum Royal 19.C.13 says that the castle is rather near Gaunes without specifying the distance, but suppresses the words beyond "en haut." The scribe could have stricken them out because he was solving disagreement of his source manuscripts (he shows elsewhere that he had more than one), or because "par devers le tertre" seemed superfluous, or because, like me, he found the reference to the "terre deserte" quite strange; to locate a castle on the lower Loire as off toward Berry is absurd. On the other hand, scribal confusion between "terre" and "tertre" is easy to understand, and is exemplified by MSS. BN 768. Its scribe first wrote "tertre"; then he expunctuated the first syllable "ter" and added a sign for "er" above "tre." The next word is "deserte"; the definite article at the beginning of the expression seems to have been "le," later rather skillfully changed to "la." In any case, near "Benoyc," which we have seen is on the Loire, a fortress called Haut Mur stands on the heights above the river, and it is seven or eight leagues from Gaunes-Thouars. Such is the location of Saumur.

F. Lot's query whether Haut Mur may have been an "effroyable jeu de mots" for Saumur (LEt 149n4) therefore appears to have had

---

[3] Distances are expressed in miles in this study except when referring to measurements in Old French. For the convenience of readers more at home with the metric system, the distances occurring in the discussion are here converted into kilometers.

miles	2	4	4½	6	8	12	15	20	22	35	40	50
kilometers	3	6½	7	9½	13	19	24	32	35	56	64	88

a basis in reality. The change from Saumur to Haut Mur follows the technique of name alteration already observed. If by Haut Mur the author of the *Benoic-Gaunes* means Saumur, he correctly describes the situation of the castle on a height. The center of the present town is somewhat downstream from the castle; so it seems that Benoic, which is "near" the castle, stands where a Saumur, somewhat smaller than the present town, was thriving in the thirteenth century.

The city of Saumur was in the direct domain of the Count of Anjou, a place of sufficient importance to be the seat of a "prévôté," as important a town as any the count possessed beside the Loire. The author could not choose an Angevin name for the capital of Ban's kingdom because Benoic was an appellation that he inherited from his source romance, the one remade by Ulrich von Zatzikhoven into *Lanzelet.*

Another circumstance lends greater credence to the probability of this location for Benoic. Let us return to the duel which took place on the meadow of Benoic between the Loire and the Arsie. F. Lot declares that "la rivière Arsie est une rivière de roman" (LEt 148*n*2). He is right to the extent that no such stream name nor any resembling either it or any of the variants offered by other manuscripts appears in the gazetteer of France as an affluent of the Loire. But we have seen how our author manufactures one place-name out of another. Now the village of Arçay is situated south of Saumur between Monts-sur-Guesnes and Thouars. It and its close neighbor, le Puits d'Arçay, are on the edge of a plain beside the Dive River two miles away. The Dive soon joins the Thouet and the united stream flows out into the valley of the Loire at the edge of Saumur, turns westward and runs parallel to the big river for three miles before emptying into it. Between the two streams there lies a broad "praerie" suitable for judicial duels. The relation between Arsie and Arçay is evident; but, even without identifying the name, Saumur's meadow is appropriate for the duel. With the castle named Haut Mur and these other facts, it is safe to accept the fact that Benoic stood where Saumur now stands.

The pages of the *Benoic-Gaunes* that conclude with the death of King Ban and the kidnapping of the infant Lancelot contain much material descriptive of the country where the action takes place. In those pages one finds the name Trebes. The name, with a change of spelling characteristic of the author's toponymic technique, is the same as that of a village that has become Trèves-Cunault on the left bank of the Loire a short distance below Saumur. The choice of the name indicates that the castle is conceived of as not far from Saumur. But it is next to impossible that the author of the *Benoic-Gaunes* should by Trebes mean the emplacement of Trèves, which is so located that for Ban in his flight to pass through country of the type that the romance describes he would have to go upstream away from any route to Great Britain instead of proceeding toward the court of King Arthur, for whose aid he intends to appeal. The description of the situation of the castle at Trebes fits in some respects the terrain at Trèves (a fact which does much to explain the choice of the name Trebes), but it differs in one respect. The river beside Trebes is comparatively small. Not all manuscripts qualify it specifically as "petite," as Sommer's text does, but it is obviously a stream of small importance as a hindrance to besiegers; rather, the marshland beyond it is the primary obstacle. Trebes castle is then not imagined as being beside the Loire.

It would be likely that the author would choose for the strong and rich castle of Trebes an important castle site, as he has done for Gaunes-Thouars and Benoic–Haut Mur–Saumur. The castle envisioned by him as the model for Trebes should be, like Ban's, part of the great lord's personal domain. Such is not the case for Trèves; it belonged to vassals of the count, and in the wars in Anjou no mention is made of its castle. If there was a castle there, it was of such minor importance that the chroniclers never troubled to record its capture, as they did for anything like a fortress. Both the location and the importance of Chinon make it deserve our attention as a model for Trebes. For Ban, Trebes is the castle "quil amoit plus que nul chastel quil eust" (III.12.39); "tant amoit de grant chierte" (III.12.31). It is an establishment provided with "riches sales" and with "esglises" and "moustiers" (III.12.35–36). As a fortress it "estoit si fors que riens nule ne doutoit au tans de lors fors afamer ou traison" (III.4.27–28). Consider now Chinon. The kings, who were counts of Anjou, were often there; "ce fut une des principales résidences de Geoffroy, d'Henri II, qui y fit des travaux importants, de Richard et de Jean Sans-Terre" (BoC 19). After Henry had defeated his brother Geoffrey and had become complete master of Anjou, "Chinon devint alors en quelque sorte la capitale de l'empire angevin. C'était là qu'on gardait les trésors du comte, et lorsque Philippe Auguste s'en fut emparé, il fut effectivement maître d l'Anjou" (BoC 20). The last phrase establishes its military importance. As further evidence on that score, it is sufficient to say that it was the center from which Henry II directed his campaign against his rebellious sons in 1173. We should not expect the author of the *Benoic-Gaunes* to use for the name of his castle a deformation of Chinon. He did not act so for Berry–Terre Deserte nor for Thouars-Gaunes. As in the case of Thouars, he replaces Chinon by a somewhat disguised version of a toponym of a place not too far away. Besides, he doubtless thought that a public acquainted with Geoffrey's pseudochronicle would assign Chinon to Kay, as the author of the *Perlesvaus* did (7824).

The topography of Trebes becomes apparent in the account of the siege by Claudas: "li castiax seoit en haut . & il sestoient desous logies . Et li tertres estoit moult ruistes et noult anieus a monter" (III.5.23–25). The situation becomes desperate for Ban, and he flees with his wife and child in the middle of the night to seek help of Arthur: "lors sen issi li rois par . j . petit ponchel de cloies qui estoit sour le petite riuiere qui desous le chastel estoit . Ne li chastiax nestoit assis que dune part . . . par deuers le tertre auoit & mons & vaus & moult males auenues . Que par la riuiere dautre part ne pooit nule gent seoir . Car li marois i estoit grans & parfons" (III.7.22–27). The description fits the situation at Chinon. There is a steep hill and, except toward the village and river Vienne, the country round about the hilltop is rough; there are still remnants of woods. The fall from hilltop to river is sharp and beyond is flat land. The "petite riuiere" is situated as the Vienne is below the western walls of Chinon fortress. The present town has in part inserted itself on the steep slope between castle and stream, but the habitations of Trebes as depicted by the *Benoic-Gaunes* are somewhat upstream. The plain beyond the river, easily flooded, was very likely marshy in medieval times. To call the Vienne in its present condition "petite" as it flows by Chinon could only be done by comparison with the Loire; but when the land beyond the stream was a marsh, part of the water volume would have been spread over a large area instead of being concentrated as in the present channel, which is in some sort canalized. Ban and his party, after a league of marshland along a "petite cauchie estroite" (III.7.28), travel through forest and over a "lande," evidently through country where they were not guided by the course of any stream. If we grant that Ban is departing from the site of Chinon, he would meet such country if he proceeded straight westward, avoiding approaches to the Loire valley and to Saumur-Benoic, which was already occupied by Claudas. He would leave the Vienne flood plain after a few miles to enter into more broken country.

He and the others leave Trebes three hours before daylight—"iij . lieues [for heures] ains le ior" (III.7.20); at dawn they reach a lake by "dun moult haut tertre . dont len pooit veir tout le pais" (III.8.2). We cannot look for the lake of the above passage north of the Loire because Ban and his party have not crossed the great river. Small lakes lying at the foot of considerable hills are found in the country a short distance beyond the south bluffs of the Loire, near Fontevrault and near Marson. The higher hill, the one which would be reached first by riders coming from Chinon, is at Fontevrault. It is some twelve miles from the old castle town. The impediments offered by the terrain, the darkness, and the character of Ban's party would naturally slow its progress despite danger during the three hours that it traveled before reaching the lake by the high hill. The need for haste seems not to have concerned Ban, since he pauses by the lake. Thus, dawn, the time fixed by the romance for arrival there, conforms to the probability that the party has arrived at the site of Fontevrault.

Leaving his family at its base, Ban rides to the summit of the hill, looks back toward his castle and sees "par tout le chastel flambe salir" (III.12.34–35). Stricken by grief, he dies on the spot. Summoned, the queen runs up to his body. While she laments him, the Lady of the Lake approaches the infant Lancelot as he lies alone beside the shore of the lake, and just as the returning mother recovers from a swoon, carries him away into the water. The hill at Fontevrault is so high that in more modern times three windmills were put upon it. From there a man should be able to catch sight of such a conflagration as Ban sees when he looks back at Trebes. The lake that the author of the *Benoic-Gaunes* knew below the hill at Fontevrault was a very modest affair, one of a string of three small ponds about a mile from town and hill; the distance explains why Ban rides rather than climbs on foot to the top of the hill. The ponds have now been drained; cup-like depressions in meadow land, out of which a water exit has been cut, bear witness to their former status. In higher, heavily forested country at no great distance, a similar series of bodies of water still exists. The pond nearest the Fontevrault hill, though minimal in area, was still appropriate to our author's aims. His lake is clearly no magic creation; he makes its reality apparent at the vital moment of the kidnapping. When the lady with her burden reaches the water's edge, she does not continue on in an ordinary manner, as those who visit the Lady of the Lake do later (III.84.23); instead she "iont les pies & saut ens" (III.14.41). Her jump is realistically described; she does not simply walk ahead.

F. Lot was almost hilarious over Braüner's place identifications. "Si on le poussait," he says, "il identifierait le 'lac' auquel Lancelot doit son surnom" (LEt 148n1). It seems to me no more absurd to attempt to locate the lake of the lady than, in the same geographic area, to investigate the place identifications of the Picrocholean war. Indeed, Lancelot of the lake might owe his toponymic appelation to two lakes, the one into which he was carried and the one where he was reared. The specification of two "tertres" in the following passage definitely implies the existence of two lakes. The lake where the lady lived "nestoit se dencantement non . si estoit el plain dun tertre plus bas asses de chelui ou li rois bans auoit este mors" (III.22.16).[4] A deception though it be, this second lake has a location; four times the *Benoic-Gaunes* mentions visitors to the lady or her retainers who arrive "au lac" (III.39.26; 84.21; 104.26; 111.33). The magic lake would naturally be not far distant from the first one but near a "tertre plus bas asses"; there is such a hill near the Etang de Marson, some six miles to the west of Fontevrault.[5]

The details related in the *Benoic-Gaunes* concerning a journey to the magic lake strengthen the probability of the provisional place assignment just made. The Lady of the Lake sends one of her damsels to bring Pharien and Lambegue from the city of Gaunes to her abode so that all may know that young Bohort and Lionel are safely housed with her. No one else can be brought. The citizens refuse to allow Pharien to leave and choose Leonce as Lambegue's companion. They and the damsel "cheuauchent tant quil vienent el chief de la valee par deuers neorrange . a lentree de la forest qui estoit apelee briosque . de chele part de la forest estoit li lais ou li enfant estoient quil aloient veoir . lors sont venu a vne iauwe qui i estoit & couroit vn petit" (III.84.2–5). Here the damsel tells Leonce that he can go no farther. But he needs quarters in which to wait for Lambegue's return. "Lors sen vont tout

---

[4] The reference to the two lakes is in the general manuscript tradition; as examples it occurs in BN 339 (fol. 2a), 754 (fol. 13c), and 768 (fol. 9d). The author of p. 65 of the *Agravain* did not understand that there were two lakes and two hills. He had Guenevere say that the Moustier Royal "est en . j . tertre et dessous en vne vallee est vns lac . Et quant vous [Guenevere's cousin] uendrois au lac si entres ens seurement et naies garde . quar ce nest se enchantemens non" (V.65.27–28). Some modern scholars have been equally obtuse.

[5] This quotation is in both the general manuscript tradition and in Sommer preceded by the words, "li lays ou ele sali a tout lui quant ele lemporta" (verified for BN 118, 344, 751, Oxford Rawlinson Qb6). Only BM Royal 19.C.13, whose scribe generally sought to amend versions before him so as to suit his own reasoning, adds "enz" after "sailli." "Ou ele sailli" may just as properly mean "at which she came out" as "into which she leaped," and the following words contrasting the "tertre" where Ban dies requires the notion of exit rather than that of entrance.

contremont la riuiere . tant quil coisissent vn poi loing sor destre le chastel de charosche qui marchisoit al chastel qui auoit non brions . si estoit la forest por chou apelee a son droit non briosque" (III.84.16–18).

Leonce is put up there and Lambegue is taken to the lake, where he and the damsel arrive in the night. The nest of proper names in the passages above furnishes one—Brion—that appears without alteration in the gazetteer of France. There seems an air of reality in the choice of the name; there is no reason for its occurrence except to explain the location of Charosches to readers of the romance and to account for the forest's name according to the procedure Dun-Issoudun. Brion is about twenty miles south of Marson, a little farther from Saumur, four and a half miles to the north of Thouars. To pass Brion in going from Thouars to Marson would be normal. The road north from Thouars comes to the left bank of the river Thouet as it nears Saumur, and follows down the bank. To go to the Etang de Marson, not far off, one would cross the stream and leave it and the highway behind. Now the village of Bron, located on the edge of the forest of Brossay, is at about the place of crossing. Here would be the appropriate point for the lake damsel's hesitation. Presumably she has not thought earlier of Leonce's lodging, and she solves the problem by suggesting a place that means some retrograde motion, acceptable to her, moreover, as furthering the mystification about the whereabouts of the "lake." The party accordingly leaves the road and goes "contremont la riuiere" up the stream, which they had just reached, and on to the castle. The time and space elements in the itinerary thus fit what would be reasonable in a journey from Thouars to Marson, and the introduction of Brion-Bron-Briosque-Brossay becomes natural; in harmony with the technique shown in Guesnes-Gaunes-Thouars, Briosque replaces Brossay, and the forest is made to depend upon Brion, somewhat, but not far, distant.

In the kingdom of Gaunes the castle in which King Bohort's widow holds out after her husband's death and after Claudas has conquered all the rest of Gaunes is named three times, twice in Sommer's text as "monlair," once "mont lair" (III.17.20; 18.27; 16.39). Variants are numerous; they throw no light on the second syllable, but tend to confirm "mont" for the first syllable (so in BN 118). South twelve miles from Thouars is the town of Airvault. Its first syllable and the definite article may furnish the needed supplement to "mont," otherwise hard to find. Its seigneur was a vassal of the viscount of Thouars, who himself had lands there (BoH 116). As with Trèves and Guesnes, the deformed name may be applied to a place not very far from Airvault. Certainly, the context is such as to give the impression that here the author of the *Benoic-Gaunes* is speaking of a place as real as Trebes and Brion. Let us consider fortresses built on "monts." The most important one in the region was some twelve miles east from Airvault at Mirebeau, where an abrupt slope rises two hundred feet from the country below. Mirebeau might well have come to the mind of the author as the last refuge of a beseiged queen, for it was there in 1203 that Eleanor of Aquitaine, supporting her son John Lackland, waited desperately to be at last relieved by John and his men after a forced march from Maine.

Bohort's queen leaves her last castle secretly as it lies under siege, and is ferried across a stream below the castle "tant quele vint en vne forest desus la riuiere qui soie auoit este maint four" (III.17.4-5); she then mounts and makes off toward the nunnery where her sister, King Ban's widow, has taken refuge. Claudas is hunting in the forest, but of all his men it is fortunately Pharien, grateful for past favors, whose path crossed the queen's. He takes her to an abbey near by, and then, when opportunity comes, has her escorted to her sister. Nothing is specified as to how long the rides are, but the implication is that the total distance is not greater than two broken days' journey. From Mirebeau to a point near Fontevrault the distance is somewhat less than forty air miles, a fitting distance for the queen's rides. A small stream in the valley below Mirebeau and ample stretches of wooded country furnish the other elements found in the passage from the *Benoic-Gaunes*.

The two widowed queens spend the rest of their lives in a religious foundation that Ban's relict erected on the hill where he died. To the Moustier Royal, Ban's memorial, "uint la roine soi tierche de nounains . & si i ot . ij . capelains & . iij . rendus . . . . Durement crut li lieus et essaucha . & les gentiex femes du pais si rendoient espesement & pour dieu . & pour amour de la roine" (III.16.18-19, 25-27).

Ban must have died on the site of Fontevrault. The resemblance between the site with the establishment just described and Fontevrault Abbey could hardly be greater. That abbey stands well up the side of a hill above the valley where the ponds lay. It was the mother house of the order of Fontevrists, to which men and women belonged but which was ruled by women. There were a few monastic establishments other than those of the Fontevrists containing both men and women, but power of government vested in the women was the order's peculiarity. The queen of Benoic evidently rules her foundation. The abbesses at Fontevrault were traditionally, from the beginning, women who, like our widowed queen, had had early experience in the world beyond monastic walls. They were of the highest aristocracy, and the nuns of the main house came of noble families. According to Colonel Picard, Fontevrault Abbey "était appelée abbaye royale" (Pic 203). It was indeed a "moustier royal" (III.16.25); it holds the tombs of Henry II, Eleanor of Aquitaine, their son Richard, and still other Plantagenets.

The geography for a limited region that has been worked out above for the *Benoic-Gaunes* has its parallel in Rabelais's use of the country about Chinon, in his account of the war between Grandgousier and Picrochole. Possibly there is a connection—ideologically as well as topographically—in the case of Fontevrault and Thélème.

In the beginning, the author of the *Benoic-Gaunes* implies that the kingdoms of Benoic and Gaunes were extensive, including most of the Plantagenet country; roughly, Benoic was comprised of the lands that Henry II inherited from his father, Gaunes of those which Eleanor of Aquitaine brought him. But when relating detailed events he seems to have narrowed the area to Saumurois and the viscounty of Thouars.

The portrayal of an institution so closely resembling Fontevrault Abbey is impressive. The author also had some acquaintance with Berry. It may be no accident that the order of Fontevrists, besides establishing many houses in the lower Loire valley, at an early date founded one—Orsan—in the diocese of Bourges. Whether or not the author of the Claudas section of the *Galehaut* volume had any connection with the Fontevrists, he certainly knew something of the lower valley, especially on the southern side in an area near Saumur.

Though the authors of the *Merlin* Continuations may not have thought of Benoic and Gaunes exactly in terms of Saumurois and the viscounty of Thouars, they understood quite well the general geography of the *Benoic-Gaunes* and conformed to it. On the other hand the authors of the *Agravain* and the *Mort Artu* had little idea of these locations; the notions of the first were vague, and those of the second were inventions of his own.

Certainly, the *Benoic-Gaunes* gains vividness from its precise localizations. But the author does not abdicate his imagination. The tiny lakes become a setting for events still famous.

2 ❦ Historical Background of *Benoic-Gaunes*

he *Death of Ban*, the *Mort Ban*, is a title that may be assigned to the first fourteen pages of Volume III (III.3.1–16.28) of Sommer's edition of the Vulgate Cycle. This chapter is practically complete in itself. The action, after an introductory page, is all contained within the area bounded by Trebes (Chinon) and the site of the yet unbuilt Moustier Royal (Fontevrault) and Benoic (Saumur). Within the chapter are concluded the story of Ban, of Trebes, and of the vengeance taken on the treacherous seneschal. The queen of Benoic is established for the rest of her days; thereafter, as the center of action, the kingdom of Benoic disappears from the romance. Let us examine the chapter to see whether there are within it reminiscences of historical events.

A similarity between the deaths of Ban of Benoic and Henry II of England is readily perceptible. Henry died at Chinon; dying Ban has just left a castle built on the same ground. Henry was buried in the abbey of Fontevrault; Ban, at an abbey located on the same hill. The close identity of the places of death and burial justifies further examination of the similarities.

The events have differences. When Ban dies, war is still raging. When Henry died, a truce with King Philip had just been concluded; at the moment there were no hostilities. Ban's grief at treason is not directed toward a person, for he does not know the identity of the traitor; it arises only from the sight of his flaming castle. Henry had known for some time that Richard his son had turned upon him; he had just learned of his beloved John's treacherous support of Philip Augustus. Ban's faithful wife arrives shortly after his death. When Henry died, Eleanor of Aquitaine was under duress by his order; she came to Fontevrault only later. There are other differences; but there

17

are likenesses within the differences already cited, and there are other likenesses too.

Newly discovered treason occurred in both cases, bringing on grief that caused Ban's death and at least hastened Henry's. In both cases war with another king, an inveterate enemy, and allied forces (against Ban, the Romans) was resulting in humiliating defeat. In both cases the king was all alone after the moment of death; in both a small party, smaller in Ban's case to be sure, soon rejoined him.

Ban, as we know, rides up to the top of a hill to look back[1] toward the castle of Trebes; "il ne lot gaires esgarde quant il vit el chastel moult grant fumee . & vn poi apres vit par tout le chastel flambe salir . si voit en poi deure les riches sales verser a terre . & fondre les esglises & les moustiers & le feu uoler dun lieu en lautre . & le flambe hideuse & espoentable qui enuers le chiel se lanche si en est li airs tous rouges & enbrases . Et entour en relust toute la terre . Li rois bans voit son chastel ardoir quil amoit plus que nul chastel quil eust" (III.12.33–40). What is here described is a conflagration in something more than a castle, in something more than an attached village. Ban is so stricken that he dies, thinking first among other thoughts that "ses fiex est teus quil ne li puet aidier ne secoure" (III.13.1–2). In Henry II's final retreat before the advancing forces of Philip Augustus and Richard Plantagenet, he paused at the top of a hill to look back at burning Le Mans. His words as quoted by Giraldus Cambrensis were: "Urbem, quam in terris plus dilexi [on this point see also R49 II.67], in qua natus scilicet et nutritus eram . . . quoniam ad confusionis meae cumulum et dedecoris augmentum mihi, Deus, hodie tam viliter abstulisti, et tibi quam potero talionem reddam, rem quam in me plus deligeres, tibi procul dubio subtrahendo" (R21 VIII.283). These words,

---

[1] In my article on Dolorous Guard I suggested that there was a relationship between the death of Ban and the fate of Lot's wife (*PMLA*, 85 [1970], 441). I should now modify the suggestion. In the last days of Henry his look back at burning Le Mans was not an immediate cause and was only a contributing cause of his death, while Ban's collapse followed at once his comprehension of what his eyes had seen, and his death came shortly. The transmutation of Lot's wife occurred as soon as she faced about, an annihilation more rapid than Ban's, much prompter than Henry's, but, as in Ban's case, a direct result of what she saw. The author of the romance does at this point seem to have been influenced by the Book of Genesis. The circumstances in the Bible are not otherwise comparable to those of the *Mort Ban*. The importance of the hill, the lament over lost possession of a burning stronghold, the solitude of the dying kings, the fall from the horse, the quick arrival of mourners, all have no parallel in the Bible, but are features common to the agonies of Ban and Henry.

blasphemous though they be, showed the same grief for the destruction of a beautiful and cherished city as those uttered at the moment of Ban's collapse. Two kings ride to the top of a hill, behold the burning of a rich and dear city, are overwhelmed with grief, and shortly die.

Ban's grief strikes him as he sits on his horse. "Se pasme . Si chiet de son palefroi" (III. 13.12–13). At Henry's meeting of surrender to Philip, soon after the retreat from Le Mans and shortly before his death, stricken by what he learned, "rex Angliae plurimum conturbatus in terram corruisset ab equo in quo sedebat nisi manibus circumstantium sustentatus fuisset" (R51 II.366).

A somewhat earlier feature of the war between Ban and Claudas at the time of the conquest of Ban's kingdom may well be an echo of the retreat from Le Mans. Almost reduced to the castle of Trebes, Ban attempts the relief of another castle still holding out. Attacked close to it, all but three of his men are killed. With the three, Ban counterattacks and drives back the enemy "tant que claudas i uint poignant tout a desroi deuant les autres" (III.4.42). Ban prays God to deliver Claudas into his hands. "Atant iousterent ensamble . si labati li rois bans si durement que toutes ses gens quiderent que il fust mors . Et lors sen parti li rois bans & fu moult lies . Car bien quidoit que sa proiere fust acomplie" (III.5.5–7). It has not been, for Claudas is soon in action again. During Henry's flight from Le Mans, he was in no condition to engage in combat, but among the leaders covering the retreat was William Marshal and among the most advanced of the pursuers was Richard the Lion-Hearted, then warring against his father. Richard seems to have thought that he was participating in a hunt, not a battle, for he wore no armor. His men came so close to the fugitives that William's party turned against them. Richard called mocking words to William, who then

> Des esperons feri tot dreit
> Al conte Richard ki veneit.
> E quant li quens le vit venir
> Si s'escria par grant haïr:
> "por les gambes Dieu! Mar(eschal),
> "Ne m'ocïez; ce sereit mal.
> "Ge su[i] toz desarmez issi."
> E li Mar(eschal) respondi:
> "Nenil! diables vos ocïe!
> "Car jo ne vos ocirai mie."
> Si feri sor son cheval lors

> De sa lance parmi le cors,
> Qu[e] il morut en es le pas;
> Unques avant n'ala un pas,
> Ainz morut e li quens chay." (GM 8835–49)

In both these episodes a defeated force counterattacks and gains a momentary victory when the principal defender unhorses the kingly leader of his enemies. Thus the retreating party can ride on to its destination.

Ban died alone on the hill where he has gone to look back. His horse comes down to his wife and her company; she sends the "varlet" who had been in charge of her son to see what has happened. On finding his lord, the servant emits a great cry and casts himself down on the lifeless form. There he is still lying when the queen arrives. Henry died with only servants present. Carrying away everything, they all fled and left the dead sovereign nearly naked. Then William of Trihan, otherwise unknown, arrived.

> Honte en out, ne li fu pas bel,
> Si le couvri de son mantel
> De bife k'afublé aveit
> Ker bien [e] cointement saveit
> Que desrobé l'orent a tort
> Li laron quant le virent mort. (GM 9159–64)

William Marshal soon joined him. In both cases a dead king died without a companion; an underling arrived, showed respect and grief in a signal and unusual manner, and soon had the support of a personage of real importance.

William Marshal was praised for many things, but particularly for his loyalty. Another actor in the romance has the same characteristic, Banin, who holds out against Claudas in Trebes. In him we may see a further likeness to William Marshal at the time of Henry's death. Banin exhibits his loyalty not only at the siege of Trebes but also in the vengeance he takes afterward on the seneschal who admits Claudas and his men into the castle. He demands a judicial duel of Claudas, and during it he kills the traitor. At the death of Henry II, the seneschal of Anjou was Etienne de Marçay or de Tours. After the king's death the poor gathered crying for alms; it was fitting that money should be distributed. William Marshal demanded of Etienne the king's money for that purpose. The seneschal replied that he had none. Said William:

> Sire, si vos n'avez des suens,
> Ja avez vos de[s] vos asez
> K'entor lui avez amas[s]ez.
> Par lui avez eü maint jor,
> Mainte richesse & maint enor. (GM 9192–96)

Etienne still protested that he had no money, neither the king's nor his own. At the moment the lords present had to accept his statement, but the *Histoire de Guillaume Maréchal* maintained that he had many pennies

> . . . en son afeire
> Les out cil muciez e repoz
> Qui respomdi par itels moz. (GM 9202–4)

Later Richard put him in prison, heavily shackled, to extract the assets from him.

There is for this episode no judicial duel in history as in the romance; there is no surrendered castle. But at the death of a king a seneschal out of covetousness betrays his trust, is taken to task by a loyal knight, and receives severe punishment under the successor to the dead king.

Etienne de Marçay or de Tours was generally disliked; he was "magnus et potens, singulariter ferus et dominus domini sui," said Richard of Devizes (R82 III.384). His enemies considered him "à la fois méchant et crédule" (BoC 116*n*1). He had military as well as fiscal functions. Just before Henry's last retreat from Le Mans, it was he who ordered that the fire be set in Le Mans (BoH 580). Henry II's aim in permitting the burning of the suburbs was to impede the enemy, but the flames spread into the city, went completely out of control, and forced Henry to flee. The king was followed only by his mounted forces; the foot soldiers could not ford the Sarthe across which the retreat had to take place (BoH 580). "Residui vero qui remanserunt de familia regis Angliae in turrim Cenomanensis se recepturunt" (R49 II.68); they held out for three days. In a tower near the north gate another group surrendered only at the end of ten days (R68 II.63). The resistance was like Banin's after the seneschal had admitted Claudas into Trebes. He and his few men surrendered only to hunger (III.10.31 ff.).

The *Benoic-Gaunes* does not blame the fire at Trebes on the treacherous seneschal; "dune cose fu claudas moult courechies que ne sai li queus de ses hommes mist en la vile le fu . Si fu la richoise des beles maisons arses & fondues" (III.9.39–41). Nor was Etienne attempting aught that could lead to disastrous consequences at Le Mans; still, in each case the calamity was the ultimate result of the act of a seneschal regarded as evil.

If there is any analogue among personages around Henry II to the queen of Benoic in the events surrounding Ban's death, it cannot be a woman, for no woman played a part in Henry's last hours. Among faithful men, William Marshal again comes to mind since, like the queen in the romance, he was the first person of importance to reach the king after death. Except for this detail, better analogies are offered by Geoffrey the Bastard, later archbishop of York, the oldest of Henry's sons who reached manhood. He, like Ban's consort, was the only member of the immediate family to attend the fallen monarch faithfully and lovingly in his hour of mortal misfortune. At his father's side through most of his last hours, he apparently was absent when the king died all alone only because the latter had caused himself to be carried into the chapel at Chinon castle for confession. The priests had completed their duties and left but had recalled only servants to attend the monarch. Geoffrey's grief was so great that, like Ban's widow, he was capable only of lamentations; William Marshall took charge. The collapse of the queen of Benoic resulted in the loss of her child. Geoffrey suffered no immediate loss other than that of his father but he ceased to be chancellor, and his troubles in obtaining the archbishopric of York soon followed.

The historical events that arouse reminiscences in readers of the *Mort Ban* chapter all took place in the provinces of Maine and Anjou in June and July of the year 1189. The order of events in history and romance is very nearly the same.

For the Prose *Lancelot* as a whole, the most important item in the *Mort Ban* is the abduction of the baby hero, which has no analogue in the events of 1189. This essential item comes from the French model of the *Lanzelet*, as does the original notion of the death of a king in flight accompanied by his wife. Despite this importance the kidnapping occupies only half a page (III.14.29–42); the *Mort Ban* is dominated by circumstances reminiscent of the tragic end of Henry II.

On her first entrance into the Prose *Lancelot* the Lady of the Lake is described only as a damsel fondling a child, uttering never a word.[2] She jumps into the lake with the boy. We learn more of her later, only after the conclusion of the *Mort Ban*. In her early history as the damsel who was taught by Merlin, she ungratefully disposed of him and is transformed from a fairy into a human enchantress, who then develops into a great lady. "Ele nestoit mie seule anchois auoit auoeques lui

---

[2] A claim sure to be raised against some of the attempts in the foregoing study to identify topography and events on the Continent is that settings and episodes connected with the Lady of the Lake are merely adaptations of locations and stories customary in fairy lore. Even if such rationalizations are present at the points questioned, the authors still might be thinking of specific spots and occurrences that they and perhaps their audiences knew. But it might be well to examine how closely or how remotely these features approach tradition.

Since the Lady of the Lake is obviously in origin a fairy personage, to find with her a lake or a hill is a commonplace. The lake into which she carries Lanzelet appears in the German romance, but the hill is absent. Indeed, the combination of lake and hill is hardly to be forecast from tradition. Furthermore, a fairy hill is ordinarily not for climbing, but there is within it an abode. The sole function of the hill in the *Mort Ban* is to serve as a point of observation, as was true for the hill on which Henry II stood to look back at Le Mans.

The Lady of the Lake as a protector of a lover has her analogues among the fairies of other tales; but fairies hovering over the upbringing of children, like the Lady of the Lake over Lancelot, are rare items, though the motif exists in the *Lanzelet*. Its development by adding Lionel and Borhort to the list of those secretly educated is extraordinary. The fairy of the *Lanzelet* does not launch her protégé into an heroic career like the Cyclic Lady, who thereby becomes similar to a protecting mistress. The closest analogue in twelfth-century literature to our fairy in this respect is Lanval's friend, who even, like the Lady of the Lake, becomes the companion of her protégé on a journey. But the journey is one of departure from Arthur's court to make the lovers eternal companions in the Other World, while Lancelot is brought by his protectress to enter an Arthurian career of worldly glory—and love for another woman.

Lanval's mistress presides over a fairy assembly in a glade. Some other Arthurian romances portray assemblies of similar derivation without making the participants creatures of the Other World; in the *Perlesvaus* the Queen of the Tents presides over one—the romances of *Laurin* and *Cassidorus* contain late examples. In the BG the glade has become a feudal estate governed by the Lady of the Lake, suggesting that she is modeled after a powerful noblewoman as much as after a captious fairy. Laudine in *Ywain* and the Queen of the Tents in the *Perlesvaus* have origins that might be similarly described, but they need a man to become their lord as well as their lover. The Lady of the Lake has no need of such support; she governs. She does not love sexually; she had rid herself of Merlin and wants no successor. She has the independence of sex that old age, nay, even maturity, gave Eleanor of Aquitaine.

It may be mere fancy, but it seems to me that Lanval's mistress, too, has certain analogies with Eleanor of Aquitaine, and her favorite son, Richard the Lion-hearted, to Lanval. Richard was certainly not poverty-stricken, but like the young king he probably thought his father niggardly. He seems, like Lanval, to have been accused of homosexualism.

cheualiers & dames & damoiseles" (III.22.4–5). She reigns over a rich domain hidden from men by enchantments. She rears Lancelot in such a household and with such an education as becomes a knight. She is usually on her estate but we see her twice on the road, the first time to convey the princes to see Leonce at the castle of Charosche. On that occasion she travels with thirty armed men (III.87.22). When she takes Lancelot to Arthur's court, her suite includes five hundred knights (III.118.35). She is always richly dressed. These two journeys provide the only occasion after the abduction in the *Benoic-Gaunes* for us to see her away from her abode. Besides being a protectress of princes she is their instructor; she discourses at length to Lancelot on the ideal of knighthood.

The Lady of the Lake is probably an idealization of Eleanor of Aquitaine—particularly as she was in her later years when, Ralph Niger says of her, "maxime novissimis diebus suis veritatem et pudicitiam [excolebat]" (RN 95). The story of Merlin's imprisonment in a cave (III.21.35) arouses a suspicion that we are in the presence of an ironic reversal of Henry's treatment of his queen. The seclusion in which the lady remains after the kidnapping—except for the two journeys mentioned—are reminiscent of Eleanor's manner of life when age somewhat inhibited her activities, and also of the existence that she led during her fifteen years under "une surveillance qui équivalait à une véritable captivité" (BoH 487). While the "Winchcombe Annals," whose last entry is for 1181, say under the year 1179, "Alienor regina Angl[iae] post longas irarum turbationes cum domino suo rege Anglorum Henrico ii reconciliata est" (Wi 137), she was usually restricted in movement. However, occasionally she appeared in places as far away as Nottingham or Normandy, was free to visit her English dower lands in 1183 (R49 I.305), and was present at the concord of Henry and his sons in December, 1184 (R49 I.333), at Westminster and London. Thus, just as the Lady of the Lake comes from her retirement at intervals, Eleanor was occasionally on the road in her years of eclipse.

In other years the most famous of Eleanor's journeys were made to convey members of her family to a new life. She took her daughter Eleanor to Castile to wed its king. She accompanied Berengaria of Navarre to Sicily for marriage with her son Richard. She journeyed up the Rhine to bring Richard home after he had been released from prison. Finally, in the year 1200 when she was in her late seventies, she brought her granddaughter Blanche of Castile from Spain to become the bride of the heir to the French throne. These journeys are of the same sort as those made by the Lady of the Lake: first, to take the young princes for inspection by Leonce; and, second, to accompany King Ban's son, Lancelot, to the court of King Arthur so that he may enter into his life of glory. Eleanor's function as a protectress under other circumstances was demonstrated repeatedly. A signal case is that of her help to William Marshal when in his youth he was wounded and imprisoned by the Poitevins.

> . . . La reïne ostaja,
> Quant ele pout, le Mareschal,
> Qui trop par out ennui et mal
> En la felenesse prison. (GM 1864–67)

After delivery

> A vis lu [i] fu qu'ore ert en l'or
> Quer la reïne Alïenor
> Li fist atorner son afaire
> Come a tel bachiler dut faire.
> Chivals et armes et den[i]ers
> Et beles robes voluntiers
> Li fist doner, cui qu'il en peise,
> Quer molt fu vaillante et corteise. (GM 1875–82)

The last line is followed by a picture of William as the perfect knight, much after the fashion that the lady portrays the ideal to Lancelot.

The most important examples of protection accorded by Eleanor were the support that she gave to absent Richard against John, and to John against his nephew Arthur. This meant participation in political affairs, a chief concern of Eleanor's throughout her life, particularly in her heritage of Poitou. The Lady of the Lake takes part in the political affairs of Gaunes, first by engineering the flight of Lionel and Bohort from the city of Gaunes, second by calming rebellious tumult through making the people certain that the princes are alive.

We have seen the Lady of the Lake active on the site of Fontevrault and permanently installed close to it. Eleanor, just married to Henry II in 1152, made a gift to the Abbey of Fontevrault through a document couched in flattering terms (BoH 354n1; PE 92; Ri 193). There were other gifts, one in 1184.

"Of Eleanor's life for nearly five years, from June 1194 to April 1199, there is little trace. . . . She was apparently living at Fontevrault in as much detachment from the world as possible for a woman of her position and temperament" (Ri 205). She was at Fontevrault when Richard died in 1199; Ralph of Coggeshall says that she was residing ("morabatur" in the imperfect tense, R66 96) there then. She was almost certainly there in retirement from 1200 to 1202, probably again later; there she was buried, though reports vary as to whether she died there or in Poitou. Any writer conversant with the area around her tomb would be familiar with her history, and thus might be led to create a character reminiscent of her. The idealization gives the impression the author of the *Benoic-Gaunes* esteemed Eleanor or was writing under the influence of other admirers.[3]

After Ban's death the personage who dominates the political narrative is his enemy King Claudas. The *Benoic-Gaunes* draws a portrait of Claudas similar to descriptions of great personages included in chronicles or like works, notably, in Henry II's case, those of Giraldus Cambrensis and Peter of Blois. The portrait of Claudas is so vivid that it creates in readers—scholars among them—the suspicion that for him there was a historical model. Bruce, for instance, says: "One gets the impression that some actual personage, so to speak, sat for this picture" (BE I.418n). Insofar as the portrait is reminiscent of great figures of the end of the twelfth century it should recall kings, since Claudas was a king. It fits not one Plantagent but several, in particular Henry II and Richard I, with occasional strengthening from the personality of Philip Augustus.

The physical features assigned to Claudas above his thorax conform too closely to the conventional portrait of a repulsive person—for instance, in *Aucassin and Nicolete*, the "vallet" searching for lost oxen —to make a contemporary sovereign rise automatically in the mind of early readers. The gigantic stature (nine feet) and the emphasis on

---

[3] Perhaps the theme of Merlin's imprisonment contains a geographic reminiscence too. The Lady of the Lake, named in Sommer's edition Nymenche, lived, when Merlin courted her, "en la marche de la petite bertaigne" (III.21.9). She put the enchanter to sleep in a cave in the Forest of Darnantes "qui marchist a la meir de cornouaille & al roialme de soreillois" (III.21.35–36). Since Sorelois, mythical though it be, was beside Arthur's kingdom (III.269), the implication is that Nymence was at times in Great Britain. Since she lived on the border of Brittany, we may conclude that she resided not far from the site of her fabulous lake at the time when Merlin found her. The territory of her activity thus seems very similar to that in which Eleanor was most frequently after her definitive quarrel with Henry; that is, in southern England, area of her imprisonment, and in her heritage of Poitou and adjoining parts of Anjou.

blackness conceal, at least partially, the realistic traits. The contrast between the head and neck described as repulsive and the handsomeness of the body introduces the antithesis later to be brought out in the good and bad "teches" of Claudas.

Behind the conventionally symbolic physical characteristics, however, I suspect that the author's point of departure was in the beginning Richard, for he, though no giant like Claudas, was tall, "staturae grandis, pauloque plus quam mediocris," says Giraldus Cambrensis (R21 VIII.248). Claudas had "le barbe rousse . & les cheueus ne bien noir ne bien rous" (III.26.37–38). Richard, says his panegyrist in the *Itinerarium Regis Ricardi*, possessed "inter rufum et flavum media temperata caesarie" (R38 I.144). This same panegyrist gives an enraptured description of the grace and might of Richard's limbs and thorax; for Claudas "les espaules les pies et tout lautre cors ot il si bel et si bien fait com len le poroit miex deuiser en nul homme" (26.40–41). The panegyrist says not a word of Richard's face, whereby we might conclude that it was not prepossessing. But for the upper parts we may turn to Henry II, who was also "subrufum" (PB 197.A). Claudas has a big face, staring black eyes, beetling brows, large mouth, and heavy neck (III.26.36–39). Henry II had a face somewhat of this sort, according to Giraldus Cambrensis: "vir subrufus, caesius, amplo capite et rotundo, oculis glaucis, ad iram torvis et rubore suffusis, facie ignea, voce quassa, collo ab humeris aliquantulum demisso" (R21 VIII.214). Peter of Blois describes his eyes in anger similarly and confirms Gerald's "amplo capite" with "leonina facies quasi in quandrangulum" (PB 197.B). It was probably the Plantagenets whom readers recognized in the portrait if they saw through the mask of physical convention.

The moral portrait reveals the same composite inspiration. Claudas is introduced early as "moult boins cheualiers & moult sages . mais moult estoit traitres" (III.3.14–15). The kings of France and England in the late twelfth and early thirteenth centuries were of such a character as to make this combination of traits seem typical of an ambitious monarch. Kings Henry, Philip, and perhaps Richard approximately fit the description, though Richard as a traitor was not so much treacherous as rebellious. Treachery is the trait developed in the portrait of Claudas: "souent metoit sus ocoison de barat & de decheuanche" (III.27.8–9). Giraldus Cambrensis says of Henry II: "verbo varius et versutus; nec solum verbi verum etiam fidei transgressor facilis et sacramenti" (R21 VIII.160). King John deserved yet harsher judgment in this respect. Philip Augustus merited no better treatment, though his treachery seems to have attracted less attention among his contemporaries, particularly after John came on the scene. Still the *Histoire de Guillaume le Maréchal*, after a page of discourse on the evil conduct of the French King toward the sons of Henry II, concludes: "Enginnié e decëu furent, Tant que par son engin morurent" (GM 8107–8). Claudas's treachery did not include betrayal of confidences; "qui son conseil li deist . ia par lui ne fust descouers" (III.27.24–25). Philip Augustus was weak on this point; his transgressions included revealing to Henry on his deathbed that John was among those plotting against him. By attributing to Claudas a virtue not possessed by Philip, the author seems to say that the portrait is meant to depict the French king only insofar as it fits all kings. Claudas's habit of promoting minor figures and neglecting the "riche" (III.27.1–3) fits an expert administrator like Henry II—Philip Augustus, too. Richard's dependence on the modestly born William Longchamp gained him reproaches (R82 I.306–7).

"Claudas fu li plus angoissos prinches & li plus auers del monde" (III.26.32). Both kings Henry and Philip might have evoked such an assertion, but again it was Henry who attracted most attention in this respect. "Angoissos" may in this context be interpreted as meaning anything between "restless" and "cruel." Giraldus Cambrensis (R21 VIII.214) and Peter of Blois (PB 198.A), among others, say that Henry II tormented his courtiers with unbounded and untiring movements. He could be clement as well as severe; but general attention was drawn to his severity by his economic encroachments upon the church, and by his punitive cruelty toward those who infringed upon his forests. "Avers" may be interpreted as "stingy" or "grasping" or both. The ecclesiastical policy just cited and Henry's skill at taxation aroused comment on acquisitiveness. William of Newburgh is as modest as anyone on this score. He says that in comparison with his grandfather, Henry I, who was also skillful at securing revenue, Henry II "in exquiriendis pecuniis paulo immoderatior fuit" (R82 I.280). Ralph Niger is venomously eloquent on the subject. For example he cries, "Aurum esuriebat, sitiebat, anhelabat, et crescenti auri cumulum vincebat avaritia" (RN 169).

Claudas "ne iames ne dounast se lors non quant il auoit si grant mestier de gent que consieurer ne sen pooit" (III.26.33–34). According to Peter of Blois, Henry deserved the opposite reputation: "nullus magnificentior in donis" (PB 198.C). Giraldus Cambrensis, however, says that he was "parcimoniae, quoad principi licuit, per omnia datus"

(R21 VIII.214). He was "largus in publico, parcus in privato." The *Histoire de Guillaume de Maréchal* attributes the falling out of the old and young kings Henry to differences over money. When the young king ran out of funds, he sent his father a request for more:

> Quant li péres l'entent, si pense
> Que il ert de trop grant despense . . .
> Li reis mande estrosséement
> Al giemble rei et a sa gent
> Feïst le mielz que il peüst,
> Que ja de rien qut il [e]üst
> Ne fereit mais ses granz largesses
> Trop par demenout granz richeces. (GM 1973–96)

From which resulted the wars

> Dunt meint gentil home morurent
> Et maint [chastel] e mainte terre
> Furent essilié de la guerre. (GM 2014–16)

Henry's stinginess was here of a kind that many fathers have felt. Words included in Claudas's lament for his son indicate that his was of the same kind: "Car ie ne fui onques larges . ne nel pooie estre de la moie main . si ne baoie a estre de la vostre" (III.59.37–38).

Claudas "volentiers aloit au moustier" (III.27.3–4). As to church attendance Henry II drew attention by his fits of piety; his penances at Canterbury are a case in point. Richard, at least after his conversion from crapulence, "mane consurgens quotidie primum quaerebat regnum Dei" (R51 III.289).

Claudas "ne faisoit mie grantment de bien a poure gent" (III.27.4–5). This was no trait of Henry II's; quite the contrary, Peter of Blois says: "nullus munificentior in eleemosynis" (PB 198.C). William of Newburgh agrees: "Pupillorum, viduarum, pauperum, in suis praeceptionibus multam curam habuit, et locis pluribus insignes eleemosynas larga manu impendit" (R82 I.282). Roger of Hoveden portrays a Richard also as charitable: "fecit quotidie pascere pauperes multos" (R51 III.29). Philip Augustus, according to the *Chronique de St. Denis*, "fu larges semieres d'aumones aus povres par divers lieus" (HGF XVII.416). In making Claudas parsimonious, the *Benoic-Gaunes* seems to have been inspired by Etienne de Marçay's stinginess when Henry II died.

I shall not try to attach Claudas's traits of early rising, his dislike of games (III.27.5–6), or choice of large horses (III.27.26–28) to a Plantagenet or to Philip, though they seem likely characteristics for all these men. The love of hunting could be considered typical of any king or noble in good health, but the terms in which the *Benoic-Gaunes* attributes it to Claudas recall particularly Henry II. Claudas "en bois aloit volentiers . ij . iours ou . iij . tout de route non pas acostumeement" (III.27.6–7); "Il amoit riuiere seur tous deduis . & plus les faucons que les ostoirs" (III.27.25–26). William of Newburgh writes of Henry II, "Venationis delicias aeque ut avus [Henry I] plus justo diligens" (R82 I.280). Peter of Blois says that Henry was "vehemens amator nemorum; dum cessat a praeliis in avibus et canibus se exercet . . . semper in manibus ejuo sunt arcus, enses, venabula et sagittae, nisi sit in consiliis aut in libris" (PB 198.2AB). Giraldus Cambrensis is at least as energetic in his comment on this point: "Venationi namque trans modestiam deditus, summo diluculo [this required early rising] equo cursore transvectus, nunc saltus lustrans, nunc silvas penetrans, nunc montium juga transcendens, dies ducebat inquietos; vespere vero domi receptum vel ante coenam vel post, rarissime sedentem conspexeris (R21 VIII.214).

In 1173, when the coalition headed by his sons was building up against him, Henry seemed indifferent: "frequentium solito venatui totus indulgens" (R68 1.373). After victory in 1175, says the *Histoire de Guillaume le Maréchal*, he found in England

> . . . deduiz de mainte manière
> Come de bois e de rivière. (GM 2389–90)

The *Histoire* does not say so, but he was making a survey of his forests and punishing those who had poached during the war. As to the analogue to Claudas's preference for falconry, Peter of Blois says (in addition to "avibus," already quoted): "Manus ejus quadam grossitie sua hominis incuriam protestantur; . . . nec unquam nisi aves deferat, utitur chirothecis" (PB 197.C). King John too was a hunter. Quotations concerning his activities in the autumn of 1206 furnish sufficient examples—again using the phrasing "woods" and "rivers" as in the portrait of Claudas. John came to England after his rather successful campaign in 1206. The *Histoire de Guillaume le Maréchal* says:

> E ala par tote Engleterre

En ses forèz e ses rivières
Qu'il aveit larges et plenières.   (GM 13308–10)

The *Histoire des ducs de Normandie et des rois d'Angleterre* says that
then: "Toute s'entente torna a deduire son cors; bois et rivieres antoit
et moult l'en plaisoit li deduis" (HNA 109). A little earlier the same
work says of John: "Toute tourna s'entente en deduis de chiens et
d'oisiaus et à conjoir la roine sa feme."

The word "manioit" in the phrase saying that Claudas "moult
volentiers leuoit matin et manioit" (III.27.5) is interpreted in Sommer's
side note to mean that he "was fond of eating." This imputation of
gluttony fits poorly with the preceding statement on early rising and
that immediately succeeding on dislike of games, both of which be-
speak ascetic tendencies; "manioit" could here simply mean that
Claudas liked his breakfast early, or the scribes may have omitted
"pou." In either case I see here a statement concerning sobriety, rather
than the contrary. Giraldus Cambrensis says of Henry II: "Erat enim
cibo potuque modestus ac sobrius" (R21 VIII.214). Peter of Blois says:
"Nullus rege nostro est honestior in loquendo, in comedendo urbanior,
moderatior in bibendo" (PB 198.C). Nor was Richard a glutton, nor
Philip.

The passage in Claudas's portrait which deals with his ideas on
love expresses nothing to be found in the lives of Henry II, John, or
Philip Augustus. Let us examine the likeness between Claudas's and
Richard's amorous conduct. It is curious that in the romance we never
hear of the mother of Prince Dorin; Claudas was evidently single
during the time of the story. We see him in a passage preceding the
portrait enjoying the favors of Pharien's wife; "Pour la grant biaute
qui en li estoit . . . claudas len ama" (III.22.34–35). In the portrait we
find that Claudas "Onques par amours not amei que vne fie" (III.27.9).
His people asked him why he had ceased loving. He answered that
love shortens life because the lover must ever be undertaking deeds so
great that the bravest man "ne poroit soffrir chou que li cuers oseroit
emprendre" (III.27.15). The author adds that during the love period
Claudas had been "de meruellouse proece & auoit eu los & pris de sa
cheualerie en mainte terre" (III.27.23–24). Claudas's single love was
apparently not that for Pharien's wife, since during his affair with that
woman he was always in his kingdom, and not "en mainte terre" doing
valorous deeds. It seems, then, that with Pharien's wife he was simply
satisfying his lust.

Richard the Lion-Hearted's disinclination for marriage with his early fiancée, Alice of France, was well known. No noble amour received notice in the chronicles; but, according to Roger of Hovedon, after the king's return from prison a hermit warned him against the evil mores that he was practicing: "Esto memor subversionis Sodomae, at ab illicitis te abstint, sin autem veniet super te ultio digna Dei." Richard did not heed the man. "Non potuit tam cito animum ab illicitis revocare" (R51 III.288). Later Richard reformed, and recalled Queen Berengaria. His marriage to her, whom he later neglected for years, was said to have been founded on early and long-continuing unsatisfied love. The Crusading period, during which the king wedded, was the time of his most celebrated deeds of valor "en mainte terre." Richard's quest of valor cost him his life before he was old; he could not last before the "chose que li cuers oseroit emprendre."

Claudas's "teces estoient & boines & mauuaises" (III.26.41); so says the *Benoic-Gaunes* near the beginning of the portrait. Similarly, Giraldus Cambrensis began his portrait of Henry II by saying "mala sunt vicina bonis, et vitia virtutibus distinguuntur" (R21 VIII.213). Claudas's traits, good and bad, not in Henry were nearly all in Richard. Philip Augustus provided a similar model but less evidently and less exactly.

Since Claudas of Berry was "hom le roi de gaule . qui ore est apelee franche" (III.3.15–16) and became a conqueror of lands later to be called Anjou and Poitou, we may suspect that some great noble was sometimes in the mind of the author of the *Benoic-Gaunes* as he prepared the portrait. One such model could have been Hugh de Lusignan, but chroniclers are not complete enough on his score to allow us detailed comparison. I believe that Hugh was too distant from our author to have provided more than a vague model for the portrait. Rather, it was founded upon personal experience with the Plantagenets of either the author or his friends.

One feature of Claudas's story as developed later than the conquest of Benoic may be interpreted as containing a reminiscence of an element in King Richard's life. When Claudas made his incognito visit to Arthur's domains, he put his uncle Patrice in charge of his own lands because his son Dorin was too wild and unreliable a character to be given the power (III.26.29–30; 28:7). On his return he learned that Dorin had acted badly (III.33.2–5). The text of the romance seems defective at this point, but it is clear that Claudas does not punish his son.[4] Similarly, Richard, on leaving for his Crusade, put his kingdom under justiciars backed up by his mother, Eleanor, rather than give power to his brother John, whose capacities for wild and unreliable behavior are well known. John acted traitorously during his absence; he received no real punishment.

In the early life of Henry Plantagenet, Stephen of Blois, king of England, was his long-standing enemy. More than one parallel exists between Claudas and Stephen. Claudas is a usurper in Gaunes and Benoic, and, at least from the Angevin point of view, Stephen was a usurper in England and Normandy. Claudas aspires to conquer Britain as well as the lands on the Continent. As a preliminary, he makes a visit to King Arthur to become acquainted with his might. There he enjoys unsuspecting hospitality. Stephen, too, before the death of his uncle, Henry I of England, was often in the king's court. He was well received but, so to speak, was there under false colors, since he was one of those who swore to put Matilda on the throne when her father should die. Claudas, after his conquest of the kingdoms on the Loire, was most frequently resident in his conquered lands, nearly always. Similarly, Stephen, after becoming king of England, lived nearly always on the island.

Claudas's only son dies—to his father's great sorrow. Though the picture of his paternal grief need have no other model than the lamentations of David for Absalom, we may remember that the younger of Stephen's two sons was unfit to rule, and that when the older son died his death was such a blow that his father, who until then had been energetic in resistance, accepted Henry Plantagenet as his heir. Claudas's grief may also be reminiscent of that of Henry I of England, who in his last years lost his only legitimate son.

Of all the royal griefs for the loss of a son, that of Henry II for the death of young King Henry, though the dead heir was far from being an only son, seems to have the closest kinship to that of Claudas because

---

[4] At Claudas's return from Great Britain, Patrice "li conte comment ses fiex dorins auoit fait maint mal en la terre . Et viles brisies & proies prises . & hommes ochis et naures . De tout che fait claudas ne me caut il . Car il a droit . Car fiex de roi ne doit estre destorbes de larguece quil voelle faire" (III.33.2–5). Manuscripts BN 118, 339, 344, 751, 754, 768, 773, and Rawlinson Qb6 read essentially the same. Royal 19.C.13 adds after "prises et homes ocis" "et done tut et despendu il ne li chaloit onques coment. De son doner, fet Claudas" etc. This version makes sense, though it still remains remarkable that Claudas ignores the statement of misconduct. It seems that the reasoning scribe of 19.C.13 amended by his own invention without filling in completely a lacuna that was still longer.

of the likeness between Claudas's lament for his son and the eulogies devoted to the young king after his demise. Here the source for the *Benoic-Gaunes* cannot be Biblical, for Absalom's character is not analyzed in detail by either David or others.

Claudas, as I have already remarked, considers his son unfit to reign while he is away at Arthur's court. On that occasion the romance says that Dorin "estoit si fiers & si desmesures & si viguereus que ses peires ne losoit encore faire cheualier" (III.26.29–30). Henry II may have spoken similarly of his heir; he did not knight him, though he put a crown upon his head. Having done so, however, he refused to give the young man power. The youth was knighted by William Marshal as he prepared for war against his father. But Henry II was a forgiving father. The young king took up arms against him more than once; Henry II always welcomed him back, just as Claudas accepts the bad conduct of Dorin after his return from Britain.

When Dorin is killed, Claudas's lament for him begins with a sentence on how great he might have been. Then we find "il ne sont en homme que . iij . choses par coi il puisse toute terriene chose mettre au desous . Chest deboina[i]retes largueche & fiertes" (III.59.3–5). The implication is that Dorin possessed all three, but "largesse" and "fierté" are the two qualities expanded upon by Claudas. Dorin had been so "large" that he made his father, basically stingy, into a generous man despite himself, so says Claudas; further: "a vostre largueche estoient tuit noiant li large qui onques fuissent" (III.59.20). As to "fierté," it was "en vous si naturelment herbergie . que nus ne vous peust faire amer homme orguelleus ne sorquidie" (III.59.24–25). "Fierté" is defined thus: "fiertes est vne grans vertus qui aime & tient chier ses amis autretant comme son cors . Et heit ses anemis sans pitie & sans merchi . ne ne puet estre la chose vaincue que seulement par deboina[i]rete quant ele la trueue" (III.59.13–16). Near the end of his lament Claudas cries that God would not have made his son such as he was "fors por moi vous [Dorin] tolir . el point ou ie vous veisse plus volentiers . & por moi faire mourir a duel & a tristor por langoisse de vostre mort" (III.60.1–3).

The young king died in rebellion; even so, his father's lamentations were extreme. Giraldus Cambrensis says: "Patri vero prae omnibus incomparabili moerore tantus dolor et tam immoderatus accessit, quod solatium respuens omne, inter duo mala perplexus, longe maluerit filium de se quam mortem de filio triumphasse" (R21 VIII.173). Henry's words have not been recorded, but various eulogies have come down to us, for the young king, despite a history of persistent misbehavior, was lamented by all. These examples, which place emphasis on nearly the same qualities as appear in Claudas's son, will suffice:

Robert de Torigny:

> Pulcherrimus facie, honestus in moribus, dapsilis in muneribus, super omnes quos in nostra aetate vidimus qui terram non dum haberet assignatam, quamvis pater ejus quindecim milia librarum Andegavensis monetae et eo amplius quotannis daret ... In officio militari tantus erat ut non haberet parem. (R82 IV.305)

Giraldus Cambrensis:

> Inermis siquidem privatusque, lenis et affabilis, mitis, et amabilis, injuriarum quarumlibet data occasione pius indultor, quantumlibet reos longe pronior absolvere quam condemnare. Qui et animum sic instituerat, ut nihil unquam dono dignum cuiquam denegaret, neminem tristem, neminem nisi competentem a se discedere dignum ducens; illum denique sibi diem, tanquam Titus alter, perditum iri reputans, quo non sibi multimoda liberalitate multos alliceret multorumque tam corda quam corpora multiplici beneficiorum largitione compararet. In armis vero rebusque militaribus galeato jam capite, sublimis, effrenis, atrox, longeque fera ferocior omni. ... Hoc unum ei votum et desiderii caput exstiterat tantae strenuitatis exercendae materiam, tanquan Julius alter. (R21 VIII. 174)

Histoire de Guillaume le Maréchal:

> Quer il esteit si entechiez
> De largesse et de toz les biens
> Qu'en lui ne faillit nule riens.
> Ha! Dex, que fera or Largesse
> E chevalerie e proesce
> Qui dedenz lui soleient meindre? (GM 6938–42)
>
> ... dedenz sei enssemble
> Tote corteis[i]e et proece,
> Debonaireté e largesce. (GM 6986–88)

Claudas's conduct with the boys Lionel and Bohort when they fall into his hands is characterized by fair promises and delayed performance. So was Henry II's in his stewardship of Alice, the sister of Philip Augustus, whom he brought up as the promised wife of Richard without ever having the marriage executed.[5] His conduct with the heiress to Brittany, whom he married to his son Geoffrey, and to Geoffrey's son, Arthur, was similar. In connection with young Arthur, John Lackland, more promptly than his father, would have come to the minds of early readers of the *Benoic-Gaunes*. After King Richard's death, Arthur, as the son of Richard's next youngest brother, was by many considered the proper heir to the Plantagenet lands, rather than Henry's youngest son, John. Arthur's cause was popular in Anjou where, upon King Richard's death, the nobles at once accepted him as the rightful heir to their county. An author with interests in Anjou would have the young prince's story vividly in mind. His readers, remembering the boy's unhappy fate, would shiver at the risks to Lionel and Bohort, delivered into the hands of the unscrupulous usurper of a child's patrimony.

A parallel recital of the part of *Benoic-Gaunes* in which Bohort's sons confront Claudas, and of the events occurring between Richard's death and Arthur's final imprisonment, will reveal relations.

Romance	*History*
1. The damsel Saraide is sent to Claudas's court by the Lady of the Lake to bring Lionel and Bohort back with her. She begins by shaming Claudas until he has the boys brought from their prison into the hall. Lionel has	1. At the death of Richard the Lion-Hearted in 1199, Arthur, aged twelve, and then free, was acknowledged as the heir to the dead king by the barons of Maine, Anjou, and Touraine. King Philip, as one supporting his

---

[5] Two more cases of child brides-to-be held by great lords for future marriage are presented by Isabelle of Angoulême and Joan, her daughter by King John. Isabelle was in childhood intended for Hugh of Lusignan, son of the Hugh who was reigning in King Richard's time. In the year 1200, when she was about twelve, John spirited her away to become his bride. With an interversion of sexes there is possibly a reminiscence of this act in Saraide's carrying off Bohort and Lionel. After a few years debate Joan was substituted for her mother as a bride for Hugh, but in 1220 Isabelle, now a widow, married him just after he had become count. Thus she displaced her daughter while the child was still in the keeping of the man who had been intending to become her husband. Joan was retained in Poitou during a dispute over dower lands. Securing her release was a major enterprise. Hugh gave her up when he was on a sick bed. The parallel to Bohort and Lionel consists merely in the difficulty of extracting heirs from a noble, retaining them for his own profit.

just learned the extent of the misdeeds of the usurper.

2. He has the admiration of the king. The latter, in compliment, offers him wine from a cup.

3. Apparently fearing treachery, Saraide equips the youths with magic protective wreaths and brooches, then bids them drink.

4. Claudas sits in full regalia. Lionel rushes upon him and strikes him down with the wine cup. He and Bohort seize upon a sword and scepter that have been part of the regal appurtenances, and use them as weapons in their retreat.

5. Claudas, who "vit bien que moult auoit de gens laiens qui ne lamoient," (III.55.35) on recovery rushes after the princes.

6. Dorin, the king's son, has come to his father's aid, and is wounded and brained so that he dies. To save Lionel and Bohort, Saraide transforms the boys into hounds and conveys them away. In turn two hounds take on the guise of boys; these hounds, turned princes, are then at the mercy of Claudas, and are not killed but captured by him.

cause, welcomed him, but the boy left him as soon as he discovered that all conquests were kept by Philip. The Breton Guillaume des Roches then (22 September 1199) took him to King John,

2. "who received him into seeming favor and peace" (N II.394).

3. But, learning at once his uncle's evil designs upon him, he fled with his mother, Constance. He was at liberty till 1202.

4. Then Arthur began war.

5. He was supported by Poitevin barons, including three Lusignans, and by a Gascon, Savaric de Mauleon.

6. Eleanor of Aquitaine, Arthur's grandmother, took up her son John's cause. Arthur besieged her at Mirebeau, which was reduced to a desperate plight. John relieved the castle and captured Arthur and the Lusignans. The latter secured their freedom eventually, but the prince remained a prisoner.

7. Claudas fails to kill them when his sword breaks on the lintel of the door to an outhouse where the metamorphosed animals have taken refuge. The king thanks God for the obstacle to his blow, for if he had killed the children, he says, "de ma main . . . si me fust reprochie a tous iours mais . & en fuisse hounis en toutes cours" (III.56.18-20). He puts the supposed children under the guard of retainers, and goes away to mourn his dead son. Fearing that his vengeance will destroy the boys, the people attack him and succeed in forcing him to surrender the hounds in form of princes.

7. John ordered that his nephew's eyes should be put out, and his party publicly gave out that the deed was done. The Bretons were furious. The order had not been executed, however. At the end of January, 1203, at Falaise, John caused his nephew to be brought before him (2, above). He "addressed him with fair words, promising him great honours if he would forsake the king of France and cleave faithfully to his uncle and rightful lord" (NJ 90-91, quoting Roger of Wendover, "iii.170"[R84]). Arthur scorned this offer.

8. Their shape is changed back and there is another attack on Claudas. Fighting ends only when all are convinced that the heirs of the dead King Bohort are alive.

8. Arthur was later moved from Falaise to a stricter prison at Rouen. His fate is not yet known for certain, though some say that John killed him with his own hand. For the present purposes there is importance in the fact that for two years no one could say whether he was dead or alive.

The similarities between history and fiction, except partially for one point, occur in the same order; a version applicable to both accounts follows:

1. A maternal figure (Lady of the Lake—Constance of Brittany) by means of a benevolent agent (Saraide—William des Roches) brings very young disinherited princes (Lionel and Bohort—Arthur) before a usurping king (Claudas—John).

2. The usurper speaks fairly to the princes, who conduct themselves scornfully toward him.

3. The protectors, fearing treachery, take measures (magic—flight) for the safety of the youth.

4. The princes, indignant at usurpation, assault the usurper (Claudas) or his dominions (John's).

5. They receive protection from others (Saraide and the passive courtiers—the Poitevins and allies).

6. A close relative of the usurper (Dorin—Eleanor) aids him and suffers greatly thereby (death of Dorin—near capture of Eleanor; she then retired and died two years later). For the parallel to history furnished by the romance, the metamorphosed dogs now replace the boys. (The shape-shifting seems to be a folk theme with no parallel in history.)

7. A first threat to the life of the princes comes to naught (the blow against the lintel—the blinding unexecuted); the notion of public protest and condemnation is connected with it (Claudas's reflections on shame escaped—the Bretons' reaction and the shame of murder heaped on John).

8. The princes disappear, and an accusation of murder is leveled at the usurper, who is never convicted of it (because it is false—Claudas; because of public ignorance—John).

Though the romance compresses the action greatly in both time and space as compared with the events of history, the parallel is certainly marked.

Bohort's rôle as compared with Lionel's in all these events is distinctly secondary. Even so, an obvious difference between history and fiction lies in the fact that Arthur of Brittany was one person and Lionel and Bohort two.

Any contemporary acquainted with the history of John's reign would perceive another parallel to Claudas's behavior toward the princes of Gaunes—that offered by the English king's conduct with the sons of William Marshal. Though Marshal had to be concerned for the fate of his own sons and not for that of the children of a former liege lord who had been vanquished, William himself played somewhat the role of Pharien. In both cases there were two youths who passed long years in the keeping of an unscrupulous king whose intentions toward them were a subject of constant anxiety. Pharien is a noble who had been exiled from the older Bohort's court. He had taken refuge with Claudas and had become his vassal. Later, he had rescued and hidden Lionel and Bohort out of gratitude to their mother when their father's kingdom fell before Claudas. He rears the fugitive children till his unfaithful wife betrays the fact of their existence and their location to Claudas. The king causes a retainer to accuse Pharien of treason (III.24.24) because "il tient vos morteus anemis encontre vous les . ij . enfans le roi bohort de gannes" (III.24.42–25.1). Pharien does not deny the protection, but maintains through his nephew that there is naught treasonable in his act (III.25.20), that it is right that he should serve both his lords. He offers to defend his stand with his body. The accuser reluctantly offers his challenge to battle. Victory in the judicial duel clears Pharien of the charge against him. Pharien has sent Lambegue, his nephew, to convey the children to their mother; but, with promises that the children will ultimately have their patrimony, Claudas persuades him to recall them and deliver them over to him (III.26.14). Lionel, Bohort, Pharien, and Lambegue are promptly imprisoned and thus held until the Lady of the Lake sends Saraide to demand the boys' release. The scene before the king and the ensuing escape have already been examined.

In the life of William Marshal there is no story of an unfaithul wife making revelations to King John. He became earl of Pembroke by marriage, at the beginning of the reign of Richard, with great territories in Ireland as well as in Wales and Normandy. In 1205 he fell into disgrace with John for having done homage to Philip Augustus for his French lands; he claimed repeatedly in open court that John had given him permission to act thus. He offered himself for judicial duel to anyone who maintained that he was traitorous; no one took up his challenge. In the same year, because of the homage done Philip, William refused to go with John to Poitou to fight the French. By 1206 John was again according polite treatment to Marshal, requiring him, however, to give him his eldest son as hostage. The next year he demanded and received the next eldest also. On this second occasion William's barons advised him not to consent.

In the meantime William was often on his lands in Ireland. There, in 1210, William of Braose and his wife, fleeing from John, took refuge with Marshal, who received them, unaware that his guests had been outlawed. The Bishop of Dublin, John's agent, demanded that the "traitor" be given up. The host insisted on safeguarding his guest as long as the latter was on his lands. Thereupon John, greatly angered, accused the Marshal in court at Dublin of harboring his mortal enemy:

> Comme il out receté celui
> Qu'il saveit qui encontre lui
> Ert [e] sis mortels enemis
> Et a sauveté l'aveit mis. (GM 14291–94)

William denied guilt; he had done his duty by one who was "mis amis et mis sire"; he declared:

> Se nus, fors vos, en velt plus dire,
> Ge sui prest de mei escondire
> Ce a l'esgar[t] de vostre cort,
> Son le jugement qui or cort. (GM 14311–14)

No baron moved on hearing these words. On this occasion four of William's friends had to become hostages for him and remained in prison a year, so badly treated that one of them died. The sons were in John's possession all this time and were released only in 1213. At one moment it was said that John intended to send them to Poitou, but the king denied it. After their release, John insisted in 1214 that the younger, Richard, still below fighting age, should accompany him in his expedition to Poitou; the boy nearly died of disease while there.

The reminiscences appearing in the romance seem to concern both situation and events. The complication of loyalties in Pharien and William are very similar, as Elspeth Kennedy perceived (Ken 92*n*). Pharien is actuated in his protection of the young princes both by his ancient feudal ties and by his gratitude to the boys' mother for a favor done him. On the other hand, he had done homage to Claudas and, despite wrongs against him, has never renounced him as a lord. His effort is always to be faithful to both duties. William's problems in loyalties began long before the reign of John. When young King Henry revolted against his father in 1173, William, who was part of the young man's immediate household by the order of the old king, was among the rebels. Marshal could argue that both contenders were kings, and that Henry II's action in putting him near the youthful monarch obliged him to follow the latter's path. Besides, the weight of gratitude was heavier in the case of the young man. William was always faithful to the crowned kings thereafter. When Richard died in 1199, he had to choose between the boy Arthur and John. His hesitation was not long, for he thought that John had the better right, but he debated the problem (GM 11867–908). Something similar arose when Philip Augustus conquered Normandy. On these occasions the problem of choice of allegiance presented itself to many men. Thereby public interest in the choice of loyalties became great in Anglo-French territory, and portrayal of the difficulties that confronted an honorable man with conflicting ties became a timely subject for treatment in a romance. In the year 1205 few attempted to maintain loyalties to both John and Philip as William did. Pharien too sought to do his duty both to Claudas and to Lionel and Bohort. In 1210 the question of loyalties was peculiarly William's. That he remained faithful to John thereafter despite wrongs done him brings his case very closely parallel to Pharien's. In both cases a noble who has incurred a king's displeasure because of double loyalties and has been accused of treason puts into the king's keeping two small boys who are ultimately released.

The events at Gaunes and the events in Ireland show kinship, though the historical facts did not here concern children. In both cases a knight, out of loyalty to one whom he can describe as his lord, receives persons fugitive from a king and keeps them for some time. Upon being accused by a retainer of the king, he maintains that he has not been guilty of treason and offers combat to whoever will take up the challenge. No one took it up in Marshal's case, and the accuser only reluctantly did so in Pharien's.

In the *Benoic-Gaunes* the events leading up to and following the return to normal form of the hounds that assumed the forms of Lionel and Bohort present an imbroglio of rebellious activity. The events are characterized by participation at the city of Gaunes of both barons and bourgeois, by frequent shifting of allegiances so that close relatives and friends momentarily become enemies, and by constant acceptance of Claudas's rôle as king. The activities are all undertaken in order to check or to promote steps that the monarch takes or might take. If we contemplate the wars and rebellions in France and England during the twelfth and thirteenth centuries, we see that the general pattern of the romance through this part conforms to contemporary phenomena. The reminiscence of a familiar state of affairs is certainly there. Very likely the author of the *Benoic-Gaunes* had in mind one particular period and scene of violence more frequently than a state of affairs extending through centuries and over many lands. I am inclined to attribute the author's skill in portraying such conditions to his familiarity with the chronic state of Poitou and with the spectacle in England offered by King John and his barons. As to Poitevins, contemporary allusions establish their reputation. For instance, the *Histoire de Guillaume Maréchal* speaks thus:

> Nostre estorie vos dit en fin
> Que tut dis furent Peitevin
> Rebelle contre lor seignors;
> Encor le veit l'om de plusors. (GM 1577–80)

Among the most factious were two men named Hugh le Brun of Lusignan, father and son, who, unlike their kin who became kings of Cyprus and Jerusalem, caused turmoil principally in and near their ancestral lands. One of the family was Ralph of Issoudun (HGF XVIII.762); Claudas's uncle Patrice was by "anchiserie" lord of Issoudun (III.28.27–31). The older of the two Hughs just mentioned may have, as said earlier, furnished the first suggestion for Claudas, and other Plantagenet reminiscences then occurred to the author because Claudas was a king.

For the rôle of the city of Gaunes the best parallel is in the part played by Limoges, especially about 1183 just before the young king died. The citizens at first received young Henry well in his last revolt against his father. The older man besieged the city for six weeks (N II.225, citing "Geoffroi Vigeois l.ii, cc. 12, 16," [HGF XVIII.216–17]) just before Easter. Meanwhile, the royal rebel and his men were extracting money from the townspeople by all conceivable means. Slipping out of the city, young Henry went off to attack Angoulême. Soon he returned to Limoges and was driven away with stones by people shouting: "We will not have this man to reign over us" (N II.226, citing "Geoffroi de Vigeois l.ii, c. 16" [HGF XVIII.217] and *Gesta Henr.* 299" [R49]). The rejected candidate retired to Martel where he died. I shall not try to establish a step-by-step parallel between Limoges at this hour and Gaunes restive under Claudas. But one or two similarities deserve attention. Claudas has aroused hatred, not by extortion of money, but by his treatment of the child princes. He is besieged in his city castle and is in danger. He slips out of the city, just how is not explained, assembles an army, and appears again before the town. There are angry negotiations but at last peace is made. Pharien and his nephew leave the city. In both cases we have the sovereign of a city making himself hated within it, going elsewhere to return with an army, and terminating the hostilities without combat and without victory.

If in these bellicose urban imbroglios in Gaunes and Limoges, Claudas is reminiscent of the young king, and if here as in other parts of the *Benoic-Gaunes* Pharien's part is parallel to William Marshal's, there is a major difference: Pharien serves Claudas faithfully only because he considers himself in honor bound by the fealty of a vassal toward his lord; in William's faithfulness to young Henry, duty was accompanied by great affection. However, William and his youthful suzerain were at outs for some time before the Limoges episode. Henry's seneschal and associates had accused Marshal of seducing their master's spouse. At Limoges the seneschal deserted the young for the old king, and William was recalled; he reached his lord only in the final days at Martel. Seduction has its role in the *Benoic-Gaunes* too. The accusation is not false, and the seducer is the monarch, Claudas. But the result is a split between a sovereign and a faithful vassal.

In a different manner Pharien's wife, like the Lady of the Lake, may have awakened in readers of the romance reminiscences of Eleanor of Aquitaine, not of an idealized Eleanor, but neither of one without some noble qualities. Pharien's wife, taken in adultery with Claudas, is imprisoned by her husband, and in vengeance betrays to the king as soon as possible the existence of Lionel and Bohort. During a street battle in Gaunes in which Pharien's usually beloved nephew becomes his adversary, the wife steps between her husband and his nephew in order to save the latter from being killed by the former. Until then she has been an unremitting enemy of Lambegue, "car par son [Lambegue's] conseil li auoit fait phariens maint anui" (III.78.35–36). She cries to Pharien that she will die herself rather than permit him to slay one who will become "le millor cheualier du monde" (III.78.38). Pharien at once rejoices that he has been spared the killing of a nephew who is straightway again his ally; "sor toute riens se meruille de sa feme qui tant lauoit hai [hated Lambegue] . & ore li estoit courue aidier al grant besoig de si grant cuer que ele sabandouna por lui a naurer & a ochire . & de che que ele en a fait a son cuer si gaaignie que de nul mesfait cha en ariere na talent que iamais maluais gre li sache . ains li pardoune son maltalent de tout en tout" (III.79.34–39).

The wife had not been mentioned between the episodes of her betrayal of the boys' existence and this heroic intervention. The only later mention of her simply states that on finally leaving Gaunes, Pharien took her with him to the estate of the Lady of the Lake where she lived on after Pharien died (III.104.34; 105.34).[6] On this occasion we are told that Lionel and Bohort had greatly honored her. Most obviously, there is in the lives of this woman and of Eleanor the story of an imprisoned wife and one intrepidly active in wars. The motivations for imprisonment were different, though several chronicles re-

---

[6] One of the functions of Fontevrault Abbey was to be a refuge for fallen women. Pharien's wife may have been the point of departure for the invention of the name Pharien—always spelled with "ph." She is an adulteress, like Potiphar's wife. The husband was thus a "Potipharien" and by abbreviation Pharien.

ported scandal in the early life of Eleanor, specifically that she had given herself to Henry II's father, Geoffrey, and to her uncle, Raymond I, Prince of Antioch. These reports originated while she was still the wife of Louis VII, whose distaste for her seems to have had multiple reasons leading him to divorce her and not imprison her. Henry II, though never fully reconciled to his wife after she had revolted with her sons against him in 1173, relaxed his harsh treatment after 1180. If he could have witnessed her conduct after his death, it might, as happened for Pharien in respect to his wife, have made him forget his "maltalent" completely. She not only championed Plantagenet interests in general; she also cooperated with at least one of Henry's bastards for whom she was reputed earlier to have had no love. Though Geoffrey, of unknown mother, "inter fratres legitimos, Henricum tertium, Pictavensium quoque et Britonum comites, naturalis ipse, non minori diligentia est et dilectione nutritus," says Giraldus Cambrensis (R21 IV.363), when he was aspiring to become Archbishop of York, Eleanor joined the party opposing him "novercali forte natura ad malum pro more proniorem" (R21 IV.373). Returning from her trip to Sicily, however, where she had brought Richard's bride to him, she stopped in Rome to obtain papal confirmation of her illegitimate stepson's nomination to the archdiocese. The parallel between Eleanor and the Archbishop of York on the one hand and Pharien's wife and Lambegue on the other is probably no accident. In both cases a woman, after she has been imprisoned for misconduct by her husband, is the declared enemy of one of her husband's closest kin, but relents and aids him.

Another one of Henry's extra-marital offspring was William Longsword or Longespee, who became earl of Salisbury. By marriage he was related to William Marshal. He married the daughter of William's first cousin, the heiress to the earldom of Salisbury. The Salisbury family presents some aspects of parallels in connection with the Pharien-Lambegue relationship.

Patrick, earl of Salisbury, grandfather of the bride of Longsword, received young Marshal into his household and took him with him in 1168 to Poitou. There Patrick was killed in a combat that has its analogies with the street fight in Gaunes which has just occupied us. On the latter occasion Pharien is leading three men, one of them disguised as Claudas, under supposed safe conduct to his tower. They are attacked by the people of Gaunes, principally by Lambegue, unable to restrain his hatred of Claudas whom he thinks he sees before him, and

by Graier of Haut Mur whom the author describes as "moult fel &
moult engingneus et preus & hardis" (III.74.38). In the combat, as
already related, Lambegue is saved from Pharien by the latter's wife; a
little later when Pharien is hard pressed and severely wounded, Lambegue comes to his aid. Much blood is shed, for no one wears defensive armor, but no one is killed. After the combat, there are those
sorry not to have killed Pharien (III.79.42), but the "loial . . . sauoient
que sil leussent mort il en fussent tenu a tous iors mais por desloial si
fuissent honi" (III.79.43–80.1).

When Patrick of Salisbury died, he was convoying Queen Eleanor
through hostile country—without assurance of safe conduct. Unex-
pectedly they were approached by a party of Poitevins. According to
the *Histoire de Guillaume le Maréchal*:

> Gefreis de Lesingnan sanz dote
> Esteit sires de cele rote,
> Qui unkes a nul seignorage
> Ne volt porter fei ne homage,
> N'unkes ne vot estre soz jou
> Toz jors i out del peil del lou. (GM 1623–28)

(Others say Geoffrey's brother Gui was the leader, but Geoffrey seems
more probable.) It may be debated whether the long relative clause in
the above verses was meant to apply to "cele rote" or specifically to
Geoffrey; in any case he is included in the characterization, which
resembles that of Graier (a parallel which I shall not develop further).
The queen was sent off toward a castle while Patrick and his men,
without time to put on their defensive armor or mount on their war-
horses, held up the advancing enemy. Patrick was transfixed from
behind; his nephew William was wounded and taken prisoner. The
queen escaped.

In both these combats we have an attack upon unarmed men by a
treacherous lot who do not accomplish their main purpose (possessing
themselves of a sovereign) and make an uncle and nephew suffer
greatly in the presence of an intrepid lady.

In this episode the youthful William Marshal plays the part of the
nephew, but the mature William Marshal furnished the model for
certain aspects of Pharien in his relations with his nephew. At these
points William Longsword provided the inspiration for Lambegue.
During part of the street combat Pharien and Lambegue are in oppos-

ing camps; at all other times they are allies. Marshal and Longsword were throughout their careers allies except at one moment in the last days of King John. Marshal was consistently faithful to the man to whom he had sworn fealty, John. There was only a brief period when Longsword sided with Louis of France; he returned to his English allegiance with John's death. Examples of the closeness of Longsword to Marshal are: When the news of the capture of young Arthur of Brittany reached the two Williams they were together; they remained together during the rest of that summer's campaign in France. On this occasion Marshal's chronicler says of Longsword,

> Qui de largesse fait sa mére;
> E haute proece et entiére
> Portent devant lui sa baniére. (GM 12126–28)

They were also close comrades in arms against the partisans of Louis of France after the death of King John. Here in both romance and history are two men with family ties, almost always allies, who were but opponents in one brief episode of partisan struggle.

The character of Lambegue shifts somewhat during the progress of the narrative of the *Benoic-Gaunes*. He is at first a fiery individual who acts impulsively and violently; he maintains the same trait to the end if faced with an opportunity for combat. Insofar, he is not unlike Longsword, who was a great warrior. But in two episodes in which he acts independently of his uncle his behavior is different. The first of these is his mission to the Lady of the Lake to see whether Lionel and Bohort were in good hands with her. The second occurs when he delivers himself up as a prisoner to Claudas to save the people of Gaunes.

For these two occasions the life of Longsword contains little parallel to the rôle of Lambegue. Among those closely connected with William Marshal, however, was one who fits aptly the character of Lambegue in its more deliberate manifestations. That man is John of Early, the prime informant of the versifier of the *Histoire de Guillaume le Maréchal*.

Lambegue, with Pharien, is made by Claudas the caretaker of Lionel and Bohort; he becomes Bohort's particular governor. Claudas chooses, to look after the children, the persons most attached to them. When King John took from William Marshal his two sons as hostages, he sent for John of Early and endeavored to put both in his charge

(GM 14538–39). Early protested that one boy was enough, and the king accepted the restriction. Both Lambegue and Early are thus chosen by suspicious kings to be governor of one of two boys held hostage.

I can cite no errand of John of Early when his particular mission was to learn the veracity of allegations and make skeptical friends certain of their truth as is the case when Lambegue goes to see whether the disinherited princes are really with the Lady of the Lake. John of Early was, however, the messenger sent by William Marshal

> . . . por saisir la terre
> E les chasteals et les citez
> Des demeingnes les fermetez (GM 11910–12)

after the death of King Richard; that is, his mission was to inform the hesitant that John should be considered the heir to Richard and not young Arthur. Both Lambegue and John of Early by their missions reassured the uncertain.

Lambegue saves the city of Gaunes from assault and reconquest by Claudas; the king is willing to desist from an attack in which he is certain of victory only when he has in his hands this personal enemy. Lambegue acts out of generosity, awakened by the spectacle of the despair of Pharien (III.100.2 ff.). Claudas is so impressed by his magnanimity that he sets him free and asks him to serve him.

King John asked hostages of William Marshal in 1210 as a guarantee that he would not rise against him. John of Early was one of those whom he specified. Early was imprisoned at Nottingham for a year, but after his release he was sufficiently in the king's favor to be offered the care of the Marshal boys. The king said:

> Que mareschal de mon ostel
> Voil que saiez. (GM 14546–47)

There was allied with William Marshal a third man with bonds toward him similar to those binding Pharien and Lambegue. This person was his nephew, John Marshal, son of William's brother Anselm. The *Histoire de Guillaume le Maréchal* twice describes him as "franz et proz et leals" (GM 17013); once the adjective "dolz" is added (GM 10764). The *Histoire* first records his presence with his uncle in 1197. The latter in 1216 had so much confidence in him that his nephew,

John of Early, and Ralph Musart were the faithful three consulted when the aged Marshal was debating as to whether he should allow himself to be named the regent of Henry III. Soon afterward the two were fighting together against the forces supporting Louis of France at Lincoln. Just as William and John Marshal, uncle and nephew, consulted and fought together, so did Pharien and Lambegue.

As furnishing reminiscences for the creation of Lambegue, nephew of Pharien, four men have been considered: John Marshal, because he was an esteemed nephew of and collaborator with William Marshal, of whom Pharien is often reminiscent; John of Early, because of his functions as child governor, ambassador, and hostage; William Longsword, because of long alliance and a quasi–uncle-nephew relationship with William Marshal, broken by one very short period of political separation; and William Marshal himself, because of his relation to his uncle Patrick, especially in a fight to protect a royal personage (Eleanor) put in their charge.

Just as the portrait and life of Claudas seem a composite of reminiscences of several kings, so Lambegue and his activities seem to reveal a composite based on the character and rôles of several men surrounding William Marshal.[7]

In the last stages of the troubles at Gaunes, Leonce de Paerne plays a notable part. When the Lady of the Lake sends a damsel to the city to inquire into the fate of Pharien and Lambegue after Saraide has spirited the children away, the envoy asks for the most "loiax hom" (III.82.8–9). She is directed to Leonce as "moult sage homme & loial" (III.82.10). Later he is chosen with Lambegue to be the ambassador to learn visually whether the children are alive. On this occasion he is

---

[7] In the *Benoic-Gaunes* the only passages of length not considered above are those taking place outside of the kingdoms of Benoic and Gaunes: the adventures of Claudas on his journey to Great Britain, and the visit of the friar to reproach King Arthur for his neglect of Ban. The comic account of Claudas's debate with his companion on the way back from Great Britain seems founded on some actual happening, but I have no notion as to what event. The appearance of a religious spokesman before a king to revile him for bad conduct would seem credible to Angevin subjects because of the Saxon zealot who expounded King Henry II's sins to him at Cardiff in 1172 (R21 VI.64–66; VIII.180–81), because of the hermit already mentioned who inveighed against King Richard's debauchery, and finally because, after Richard was buried at Fontevrault, King John, who was still at the abbey with Saint Hugh of Lincoln, was roundly chided by Hugh for his misbehavior during a sermon there (See K 348 for an account rather accurately summarizing that in the *Magna Vita Hugonis*, R37 283 ff.). This last incident may have been personally witnessed by the author of the *Benoic-Gaunes*, certainly by Eleanor of Aquitaine, who was also at Fontevrault.

described as "li plus riches hons de tout le regne & li plus loiax . et auoit este cousins germains au roi bohort . . . & estoit bien de leage de . 1 . ans ou de plus" (III.83.37–39). His caution is great. When the Lady of the Lake brings the princes to Charosche Castle, he rides toward them with a messenger sent to inform him of the approach of the cavalcade, but "moult se doutoit de traison" (III.87.30), and he insists that Lambegue come personally to reassure him. He is perspicacious enough to guess the identity of Lancelot, whose origin the Lady of the Lake keeps secret. He is at the head of the embassy of ten notables who go to treat with Claudas concerning the surrender of the city. In the negotiations he demonstrates how completely "loial" he is by refusing to deliver Lambegue to Claudas or even the three hostages whom the king has committed to Pharien's personal care.

The characterization of Leonce is thus totally complimentary. Since he is the "richest" man in the region, and Gaunes is situated where Thouars is, there would seem to be some identification with the viscount of Thouars. Almery, who was viscount during the reign of King John, has been characterized by Kate Norgate as a "veteran turncoat" (NJ 201). He scarcely deserved the epithet, for he was more faithful to John than most, yielding to Philip Augustus only when immediately confronted by that king in 1205 and 1214. But he hardly displayed the steadfastness which Leonce exhibited before the imperious demands of Claudas. We may say that Leonce was reminiscent of him only vaguely.

If we examine Leonce's function as an ambassador the most striking element in it is that the displaced but rightful possessors of the throne of Gaunes are brought to him from a distance, that there is a joyous reunion, and that he never penetrates into the fastness where the princes have been living. To my mind there is a similarity here to the circumstances accompanying the liberation of Richard the Lion-Hearted after his imprisonment in Austria. When news of Richard's imprisonment reached England, as told by Kate Norgate, "Bishop Savaric of Bath [went] to treat with the Emperor, and the abbots of Boxley and Robertsbridge to open communications, if possible, with Richard himself (Howd iii.197–98 [R51]); this, however, was a difficult matter, for, of the place of his confinement, nothing was known except that it was somewhere in the Austrian dominions and these were to most Englishmen of that day a wholly undiscovered country. . . . They met Richard at Ochsenfurt on his way to be delivered up on Palm Sunday to the Emperor Henry at Speyer (Howd iii.198 [R51])" (N

II.324). So far we have a parallel to Lambegue's visit to the lake. Later, when Richard was about to be freed, he called for his mother. After faithful service to him during the period of his disappearance, she now became a delegate from his people to greet him and to make sure his ransom was delivered. She met him at Mainz at some distance from the mysterious land of his incarceration. The parallel in action between Eleanor and Leonce at this point is evident. In addition there is for both an accent of age (Eleanor is seventy; Leonce, fifty or more). We need not be surprised that nobility of character is attributed to a person analogous to Eleanor, for the same idealization occurs in transforming the queen into the Lady of the Lake. It is curious in the *Benoic-Gaunes* to see one fictionalization of Eleanor (Lady of the Lake) meet another (Leonce). That reminiscences of Eleanor and Almery should be joined in the concept of Leonce is not surprising, because these two were allies working for John's cause when Arthur's adherents were threatening.

The use of historical reminiscences is perceptibly different in the *Mort Ban* from what it is in the rest of the *Benoic-Gaunes*, which I shall label the *Pharien*. In the *Mort Ban* the events very nearly correspond item for item in chronological order to the events in Henry II's last days, and except for the multiple roles of William Marshal the characters correspond nearly person for person.

In the *Pharien*, on the other hand, only Pharien himself can consistently be referred to one man, William Marshal. The fictional characters of Claudas and Lambegue seem composite portraits made up of traits drawn from several men known to us through history. Contrariwise, Eleanor of Aquitaine's rôles in several historical events seem to have furnished the inspiration for more than one individual in the romance—the Lady of the Lake, Pharien's wife, and Leonce. In dealing with events the same mingling of reminiscences exists. In general the resemblance of incidents in the romance to actions in history are complicated, extending without chronological order over a period from 1183 to 1216. The most important fictional episode, the visit of Saraide to Gaunes to bring away the disinherited princes, seems to be inspired essentially, particularly chronologically, by the last days of young Prince Arthur. There seems to be in the episode an admixture of reminiscence of the circumstances of Richard's release from prison in the Empire. In several other ways events affecting William Marshal and his sons appear to be reflected; in the case of Montlair, there seems to be a reminiscence of Eleanor besieged at Mirebeau.

The key historical figure furnishing inspiration to the author of the *Benoic-Gaunes* is William Marshal. Not only are events often referrable to his biography, but the most important ideological theme running through the romance concerns the same *cas de conscience* as that which repeatedly confronted Marshal; that is, the demands of an ideal of loyalty under delicate circumstances. The problem of loyalty is concentrated in one man in both history and romance. The historical personages forcing Marshal to make difficult decisions were several. Probably Claudas is made to be reminiscent of several kings in history, because the problem-makers must be summed up in one man confronting Pharien, the embodiment of loyalty. Lambegue is similarly the fictional concentration of all the men surrounding Marshal who stood in a relationship of affectionate subordination to him. As inspiration William Marshal remains outstanding in the *Pharien*.

In the *Mort Ban*, Marshal also has his analogue in fidelity—Banin. To assign to King Ban himself the parallel to William Marshal's unhorsing Richard is in no way to weaken William's importance as a source of fictional inspiration. The whole *Benoic-Gaunes* seems to have been written by a man who admired William Marshal, the great earl of Pembroke.

That man also admired Eleanor of Aquitaine, as the reminiscences of her in the romance demonstrate. Her figuration as the Lady of the Lake hovers over the whole of the Prose *Lancelot*. Her figurations in the *Benoic-Gaunes*, taken together, represent her as a woman with a past (beloved by Merlin and seduced by Claudas), at moments vindictive, but powerful, wise, active, and almost always protective.

Women in the general life of mankind as portrayed in the *Benoic-Gaunes* have greater importance than in other romances of the period. Except for the spiteful revelation of the existence of the princes by Pharien's wife, they behave laudably.

The geography of the *Mort Ban* concentrated on Fontevrault and its abbey; and in the *Pharien* the rôle played by women and the admiration displayed for the abbey's patroness, Queen Eleanor, makes a tie between the *Benoic-Gaunes* and the abbey highly likely. The possibilities of a relation between William Marshal and the Fontevrists cannot be divined from the *Benoic-Gaunes*; we must seek elsewhere for evidence of such a connection.

From the knowledge of the local terrain, which he describes so accurately, the author of the *Benoic-Gaunes* was apparently bred in the region on the border of Anjou and Poitou, most likely in the viscounty of Thouars. He must have been something more than a monk at

Fontevrault; apparently he passed his life at various places in the Plantagenet holdings. His intense interest in political ideas and the breadth of his picture of human activity indicate that he was by no means a recluse.

3 ❦ Historical Background of *False Guenevere* and *Claudas-Frolle*

he episode of False Guenevere near the beginning of
Sommer's Volume IV must occupy us because of its
historical reminiscences. In it the geography is largely
fanciful, though the placing of Carduel at four days' journey from
Camaalot, and then implying that Camaalot is "de Logres la cité,"
suggests that Carduel and Camaalot stand for Caerleon (or Cardiff)
and for London (or a spot near it). The location of Bedingran, Sorelois,
Gorre, and Carmelide remains, however, completely vague.

In the Prose *Lancelot's* False Guenevere tale the folk theme of the
substituted wife takes a form that resembles other versions, primarily
in the fact that there is a substitution brought about by a malicious
woman and an accomplice, with the husband hoodwinked to the point
of thinking that the woman whom he accepts for a period is the one he
intended to marry. To an extent tradition doubtless determined
this part of the Prose *Lancelot*. The particular source is probably a
version of the story of *Berthe au grand pied*, similar to that preserved
in the *Saintonge Chronicle* (1225). The Arthurian version has many
features differing from tradition. I shall mention only two as a justification for not attempting a further comparison with the Berthe version or folklore stories. False Guenevere, instead of turning up at the
time of the marriage as is the usual tradition, presents herself many
years after the date of the marriage. The accomplice is an old man
instead of a woman. Such innovations can be explained as reminiscent
of events comparatively recent at the time of composition.

The utilization of the Pope's interference with Philip Augustus

55

when the king put away his wife, Ingeborg, is even plainer in the *False Guenevere* than when Arthur takes back his mate in the *Mort Artu* (cf. p. 85); in the *False Guenevere*, as happened with Philip, a second wife immediately replaces the first for a period of some length. The similarity between fact and fiction was first noted by Freymond in 1892 (ZRP 16 [92].97*n*). Papal interference occurs, however, only in the long form of the *False Guenevere*.

Reminiscences of False Baldwin of Flanders, no fictional character, also exist; many of these are found in both the short and the long forms of the *False Guenevere*. After the Crusaders had captured Constantinople from the Greeks, there was war with the Bulgars. Emperor Baldwin, in a campaign against them, was taken prisoner in 1206 and never heard of again. In the spring of 1225 an old hermit was discovered in the Glançon Wood in Flanders who was said to be the Emperor Baldwin of Constantinople. For some time after the hermit had been found, he denied that he was Baldwin, then finally admitted it. He told a story of escape from the Bulgars with help from a lady of that nation whom he later abandoned, of enslavement by other barbarians, of release by German merchants, and of turning hermit to atone for his sin against his Bulgar liberator. The old pretender was generally acknowledged as authentic by the people of Flanders, including nobles and burghers, for a few weeks in the late spring. Countess Jeanne, the daughter of the true Baldwin, was not among the deceived, and took refuge in Paris. Louis VIII at Péronne, before an assembled court, received the pretender in state, and after affabilities began asking questions. The impostor could not remember when he had first done fealty to the king of France. He was identified by the bishop of Beauvais as a jongleur who had been in his prisons. He fled from the court through Flanders and disappeared, supposedly on the way to Cologne. He was later picked up at a fair in Burgundy and turned over to the Countess Jeanne. Shortly, he died; he had probably been executed. There was no general punishment for the desertion of the countess.

In the *False Guenevere* an impostoress, with a dignified old man, Bertholai, as her chief and constant aid, convinces the people of the kingdom of Carmelide that she is the true Guenevere (IV.45.10). Bertholai and a damsel submit her claim to Arthur; the old man offers to uphold it in battle. He is rejected with scorn as a combatant (IV.16.10). Arthur sets a formal hearing before court for a later date. The pretenders, seeing a hopeless case unless they win Arthur over, lure him into a forest after a boar and imprison him (IV.47.37). The charmer successfully seduces him when she has him to herself (IV. 50.12), and then comes back with him to the court of Logres. There is another hearing and Arthur maintains that the barons of Carmelide must decide who is the true Guenevere (IV.56.2). They decide for the impostoress, and Arthur accepts this judgment. For Arthur's erstwhile queen, Bertholai announces a sentence of disfigurement (IV.58.38–59.2). The barons of Logres object, and in the lists Lancelot victoriously defends his beloved against three knights of Carmelide. Before the court Lancelot's friend Galehaut had been the true Guenevere's constant champion. After the judicial combat she is allowed to depart for his kingdom of Sorelois (IV.72.4). Shortly the Pope interferes, causes Arthur to be excommunicated, and puts "toute la terre de la grant bertaigne en escommeniement . xxi . mois" (IV.73.2–3). The two impostors become paralyzed and their feet begin to rot away and stink. The hermit Amustans, whom Arthur meets in a period of anxiety brought on by these circumstances, besides acting as a preacher, says, "se iou ooie lune et lautre parler . et iou parlaisse a elles . ij . iou sauroie tost laquele fust ta droite femme . quar iou fui norris denfance en lostel le roy leodegan . Et si sai asses denseignes de la royne genieure sa fille . qui sont priuees entre moi et li que nus ne set fors que nous . ij ." (IV.77.22–26). Without making use of this ability to identify, Amustans finally persuades the pretenders to confess their crime publicly (IV.80.5). They are not executed but die. The barons of Carmelide went to Sorelois to beg forgiveness of Guenevere, their queen, who grants it (IV.81.30).

The above analysis is a résumé of the long form of the *False Guenevere*. The essential difference between the two forms is that in the short one, after the judicial combat, the impostors are considered false and are burned.

The differences between the *False Guenevere* and the historic episode of the False Baldwin are great enough that no continuous parallel can be drawn, but there are so many resemblances as to leave little doubt as to the occurrence of reminiscences. The resemblance that runs through both the long and short accounts, in addition to the basic fact of fraudulent claims, is that the pretender is supported by the people of a quasi-independent state (Flanders-Carmelide) under the suzerainty of a somewhat distant powerful king (Louis VIII-Arthur) and that the court of the major kingdom (France-Logres) is from the beginning resistant to the claims. The lady, who is the rightful mistress of the secondary state, is rejected by her people, and takes refuge in a friendly court. Later the lady graciously accepts the remorse of her subjects.

The insistence upon the rôle of Bertholai throughout the career of False Guenevere is strange. He is, so to speak, the other half of a single unit, the impostor. His accomplice acts independently only in the seduction of Arthur. He appears without her only as her spokesman before the court. As an impostor he enjoys an importance quite reminiscent of False Baldwin's. Also in both cases the emphasis on age is marked. Bertholai's first appearance at Arthur's court when he is rejected scornfully is reminiscent of False Baldwin's appearance at Péronne. False Baldwin made no oral confession, but his ignominious flight from Péronne was as clearly as speech an admission of his fraud. The confessions of Bertholai and his accomplice, followed by a miserable death, recall the end of False Baldwin.

Arthur in the *False Guenevere* resembles Louis VIII in that he presides over the court that makes decisions. Because the decisions in these cases are so opposite, it is not surprising that the kings' resemblances are slight. The part that Galehaut plays in the queen's affairs has rather the echoes of King Louis's behavior. Both Louis and King Galehaut give refuge in their lands to the distressed ladies. Both stand forth as powerful skeptics. A signal difference between them is that Louis, instead of being the dear friend of the lady's natural champion, was the arch enemy of Jeanne's natural protector, her husband, Ferdinand, who had been captured and imprisoned after the battle of Bouvines. In the *False Guenevere* the rôle of dear protector was there to fill, and Lancelot fell into it as a matter of course, particularly since in a romance the episode without a judicial duel would have been unthinkable; the doughtiest of knights must help the wronged woman. Aught else would be unthinkable when the lady is Queen Guenevere and the knight is Lancelot.

The sequel to King Arthur's boar hunt in the *False Guenevere* recalls in certain respects the disappearance of the true Baldwin and the beginning of the Bulgarian adventures invented by False Baldwin. Both monarchs were captured and carried off alone so that their people did not know what had become of them. The general consternation and search for a successor was the same in both cases. Gawain, as the king's nephew, was drafted to succeed him. Baldwin's brother Henry became his successor. The state of Arthur's subjects also recalls that of the adherents of Richard the Lion-Hearted, who was lost and then imprisoned. The False Baldwin's claim to have been freed through the

love of a Bulgar lady stands parallel to Arthur's seduction by False
Guenevere and his liberation when she has made him obedient to her
will. The story here invented by False Baldwin shows no originality.
Liberation of prisoners because of affection aroused in a female among
captors is a commonplace story and not unknown to history. The significance here is that the motif is fitted into two stories of deception.

The rôle of Amustans recalls that of the bishop of Beauvais. There
seems no reason to provide the Arthurian hermit with an unused
power to identify the impostors except as a reminiscence of what happened at Péronne. Both churchmen bring about the public revelation
of the substitution plot.

If the short form of the *False Guenevere* is considered the essential
form, the parallels to Amustans and some of those to Galehaut disappear. Those that remain are much more important than those
stricken out; for instance, the rejection of the fraud after discovery
before an assembled court is still present.

Recognition of the reminiscences between the *False Guenevere* and
the episode of False Baldwin sets a *terminus a quo* for the composition
of this part of the romance—1225. Few would deny the existence of
reminiscences because of this date. There is also an implication that the
author was well acquainted with the historical affair, not so much
because he knows that the fraud existed as because of his insistence
upon all the procedures of the court.

The part of the *Agravain* that recites the final war against Claudas
(V.323-77; Introduction 256-63) is a section of the work independent
of the rest. Let us call it the *Claudas-Frolle*. We have seen in the
Claudas-Frolle that Flanders and Gaule are situated toward Great
Britain from Benoic and Gaunes, but the geography is otherwise ill-
defined. It will be no surprise, then, to discover that one reminiscence
of contemporary wars is sharply evident, while others are less salient.

The discussion that follows assumes that the man who wrote the
Claudas-Frolle was, as a contrast to the authors of the *Benoic-Gaunes*
and the *Mort Artu*, a Francophile. The justification of the assumption
will become evident without formulation, but F. Lot has already shown
the writer's Gallic patriotism (LEt 184-85).

The Francophile imagines Arthur in rôles similar to those of a
French king. The most obvious example of Arthur so behaving is in
the combat with Frolle d'Allemagne (V.370 ff.). The conversion of
Frollo, who was a tribune in Rome in Geoffrey's *Historia Regum
Britanniae* and in Wace's *Brut*, into a German with no Roman con-

nections in the *Claudas-Frolle* (in the *Mort Artu* one is mentioned, 160.59; see further p. 102) seems to satisfy a patriotic need. In conquering the German invader, Arthur behaves like Philip Augustus fighting Otto at Bouvines. We have already perceived that Claudas, when usurping from the sons of King Bohort, is reminiscent of King John displacing his nephew Arthur. In the *Claudas-Frolle*, Claudas again recalls John, but as we shall see, John in his last days in England.

The trigger in the *Claudas-Frolle* for the Britons' undertaking the campaign against Claudas is Guenevere's sense of insult when Claudas with abusive words refuses to release an imprisoned messenger of hers. Lancelot's wrath at the usurpation of his heritage is thereby kindled so that he advocates the campaign, and Arthur and his barons accept the proposal. Lancelot is not, however, the representative of legitimacy in the expeditionary force; Bohort and Lionel are its leaders under Gawain.

Readers in the thirteenth century would recall Louis of France and his invasion of England. History provides no incident like Guenevere's provocation, but a woman entered into Louis's motivation. Blanche of Castile was the granddaughter of Henry II, and thus she furnished to her husband, Louis of France, the basis of his claim to be rightfully displacing the usurper, John. Louis, then, by delegation from Blanche, was rightful heir, like Bohort and Lionel. Blanche, like Lancelot and Guenevere, remained in the land of her adoption. Not all the threads in this snarl of reminiscences would probably come to the mind of a thirteenth-century reader, but the parallel of a sovereign furnishing forces for a close relative to cross water for invasion of a claimed heritage is evident enough.

Claudas, faced by the threat of invasion, fears that the people will desert him (V.329.11 ff.). He offers to allow the departure of those unwilling to support him. There is an exodus. Afterward, "Sire fet . i . sen parent . sire io ne quid pas quil uus soit [remes] de cheualers & de serianz pas . ii . c." (V.331.2–4). Claudas accumulates forces by sending out word in and beyond his domain, and becoming "si larges & si cortois que tuz li mundz len proisoit" (V.331.11). The situation which John faced before Louis's prospective invasion was similar. He did not need to tell the unfaithful to leave; many were already in rebellion. Like Claudas, he found himself largely deserted, and he sent abroad and assembled a force of well-paid mercenaries, particularly Flemings.

Gawain and his army land in Flanders and vanquish its count.

Then, without meeting resistance in Gaule, whose leader had died, they proceed on to the kingdom of Gaunes. The Flemish victory of Gawain has its closest analogue not in the events of 1216 but in the state of Flanders in 1214 in the Bouvines campaign and afterward. The unresisted march across Gaule is parallel to Louis's scarcely resisted triumphs as he went from his landing through London on into western England.

In the romance there may well be reminiscences of specific campaigning in the successful surprise attack upon the approaching men of Great Britain, in the pitched battle later, in the siege of Gaunes and the defeat of the attempted surprise attack by the relieving Roman army, even when supported by a sortie from the besieged city, and in the declaration of a truce; but it is sufficient to say that these occurrences seem selected samples of the typical military action during the period in which the pseudo-Map Cycle was composed.

At the news of approaching reinforcements for his enemies Claudas flees, to appear no more in the Cycle. His withdrawal in collapse cannot be said to be typical of the rest of his career, quite the contrary; and there seems in his behavior a reminiscence both of the death of John in precipitous retreat and of the flight of Otto of Brunswick after the battle of Bouvines.

Except in this conclusion of the *Claudas-Frolle* and in the defeat of the Flemish near its beginning, the analogues in the romance to the efforts of Louis against John in England and to the triumph of Philip Augustus against the allies at Bouvines are well separated by making the first apply to Gawain's forces and the second to the army led by Arthur. The two exceptions are at the beginning and the end of the campaigning in the romance. As for an explanation in the latter case, it was necessary, in view of the source of the author of the *Claudas-Frolle* in the *Historia Regum Britanniae*, to depict Arthur as slaying Frolle; but the author could not omit an allusion to Otto's ignominious escape from Bouvines to further misfortunes. Therefore Claudas, contrary to his stubborn wont, must flee like Otto. Since Arthur with Frolle is reminiscent of Philip Augustus with Otto, it may be expected that Arthur's behavior should be similar to Philip's under other circumstances. The proper heirs to Benoic and Gaunes have already well-developed plans before they speak of the Continental venture to King Arthur. He approves but stays home during the campaign before Gaunes. Similarly, Philip allowed Louis to proceed as he liked with the invasion of England, approving of the project but remaining a spectator. Arthur insists that Lancelot should not accompany his cousins and Gawain; he should remain with him: "Uus me lerrez lancelot pur fere compaignie & pur garder ma terre" (V.327.9–10), he says. While the forces before Gaunes were struggling, Lancelot was enjoying life. After seeing off the expeditionary force, "li rois sen returne & lancelot ouec li . si moinent la meilleur uie quil porent & la plus ioieuse ne il nest ioie del secle que lancelot ne eit . . . & se lancelot a bone uie del roi . encore a il meilleur de la roine . quar ele ne li uee a fere ren quil uoille fere de li" (V.336.29–34). Lancelot's passivity while others are fighting for him is curious. Nor does he play any great part when Arthur leads reinforcements to Gaunes. How shall we explain his acceptance of luxury at such a time? I have already suggested that Guenevere at this time is reminiscent of Blanche of Castile. It is most doubtful that Blanche deserved the reputation; but she passed for the paramour of Thibaut de Champagne, a stripling supposed to have gained the favors of the older woman. The author of the *Claudas-Frolle* seems to have found Lancelot reminiscent of Thibaut; and, no partisan of the count of Champagne, he made of Lancelot a *fainéant* contrary to all tradition. There is no hint of condemnation of Lancelot. The words of praise are numerous as ever; he simply becomes a spectator rather than a participant, after instigating action at Guenevere's behest.

The probabilities are strong that the author of the *Claudas-Frolle* wished to attract readers by the parallels to contemporary life that he introduced. His public, still mindful of the Battle of Bouvines, would have been at once alerted by the qualifying element of Frolle's name, d'Allemagne. Thus alerted, his readers could hardly have failed to recognize, first, the implications of the humiliation of a German recounted in almost jocular fashion,[1] and thereafter, the parallel to the exploits of Louis of France.

---

[1] Ferdinand Lot says that "l'humour est quasi absent de l'oeuvre" (LEt 276). The allegation is refuted by the first part of my *n*7, ch. 2. Also, the author must have been consciously attempting humor in the *Claudas-Frolle* section. The jocular tone in the account of the duel is evident, if not elsewhere (and it is elsewhere), in the last phrase of this sentence: "Lors commencha frolles moult a lasser quar moult sestoit tout dis hastes de ferir sour le roy artus . et maintes fois li faisoit li roys falir de gre" (V.374.11–12). In the *Claudas-Frolle* there is comedy of situation as well; the author must have known that it is funny to have a piqued woman urge on a lover to urge on his cronies to urge on a king to embark on war, and then to have the woman, the lover, and the complacent king stay home as a joyous *ménage à trois* while the others rode off to noble deeds. There are other examples of humor in the Cycle, almost always deadpan, making one

suspect that the author and a penetrating few were smiling while the naïve sat enraptured. One example is the conduct of the lord of Dolorous Guard in and after his flight; he is downright ludicrous when he rides into a river (just as Lancelot was in Chrétien's *Charrette*, under similar circumstances). There is certainly comedy of situation in the *False Guenevere*, even in the *Mort Artu*, when Arthur takes back his wife. Perhaps at that point the author wished no one to perceive it, but he seems to have meant everyone to enjoy Gawain's discomfiture when rejected by the Maid of Escalot: "Quant messire Gauvains entent cele qui se fierement s'escondit, si li respont trop corrouciez" (26.54–55).

4 ❦ British Geography in the Prose *Lancelot* and the *Mort Artu*

hen the Lady of the Lake takes Lancelot to Britain to present him at Arthur's court, her party lands at Flodehueg (III.118.41). F. Lot, evidently convinced that the author had a real locality in mind, says: "Je n'ai pas su l'identifier. Le premier terme est celui qui termine les noms de Harfleu(r), Honfleu(r), Barfleu(r), Fiquefleu(r); il correspond au scandinave *floedh.* . . . On le retrouve en Angleterre" (LEt141*n*1), and he names Ebbsfleet. The sense of the word "fleet" here displayed is that of "creek," "inlet," "bay." I agree with Lot on the presence of the word in Flodehueg. Indicating geographical conditions consonant with those conveyed by "fleet," several names of towns on the English Channel end in "mouth."

Among the town names so terminating is Weymouth; the lagoons to the west of it are called "fleets." "Wey" and "hueg" seem sufficiently related to suggest that the author, using the technique for name alteration displayed in the *Benoic-Gaunes,* turned Weymouth into Flodehueg. The port is located at a favorable landing point for ships that have sailed from Continental harbors to the west or south of Normandy. There is nothing in the romance to indicate where embarkment takes place, but, since the party has begun its journey near Saumur, departure from the Nazaire-Nantes area or from La Rochelle seems natural; the reader may remember that the authors of the *Merlin* Continuations choose La Rochelle.

From Flodehueg, four days' journey takes the Benoic party to Lavenor within twenty-two English leagues of Kamaalot (III.119.2–5). Because, by the next day at five o'clock, the travelers have covered twenty of those leagues, the reader may presume that for the author of the passage an English league was equivalent to a mile. The number of days spent on the road and the distance normally covered in one day yield enough detail to suggest definite localities. The distance from Flodehueg to Kamaalot as measured by these days of travel seems to correspond rather well to the mileage from Weymouth to the neighborhood of London. Still, since the romance says nothing as to the direction of the journey, Kamaalot might be anywhere about one hundred miles from Flodehueg on an arc from the Welsh border to London.

With a beginning so well provided with details on travel in Britain, we might hope to find many clues to the geography of the land. But after Lancelot is delivered to Arthur (III.122) the topography of the Prose *Lancelot* becomes vague. The castle of Dolorous Guard is near the Humber; only in the case of Caerleon do we learn the castle's distance from any other place. The messenger bearing the news of Lancelot's capture of Dolorous Guard leaves the castle on a late afternoon and on the third day before evening he arrives at Caerleon (III.153.28). From Hull to Caerleon is more than 175 air miles; thus, the messenger has covered more than fifty-five miles a day, partly over rough terrain. We must conclude that the author of the pages on Dolorous Guard was not well informed on distances in this part of England. Nowhere else in the last three-fourths of Sommer's Volume III do we find commitments that connect fictional placements with reality. And, as others have pointed out, there are absurdities, such as locating "Windesores" by a "petite" river (III.333.39).

Without examining the details of Sommer's volumes IV and V, let us assume that the topography of Great Britain is as neglected in them as in the latter part of the *Galehaut*, that even when the authors have certain towns or districts in mind they make no effort to form a pattern of space relationships, either fictional or real. Certainly, in the *Queste del Saint Graal*, once out of Kamaalot, one has little knowledge and less concern as to the distances from one scene of action to another. Lancelot's voyage that finally ends at the Grail Castle seems sometimes on a lake, sometimes on a river, sometimes on the sea along the coast. Perceval's locations change in an equally dream-like manner. But the last part of the pseudo-Map Cycle, *La Mort le Roi Artu*, brings back a world where space is measured.

In *La Mort le Roi Artu*, Lancelot, leaving Logres—that is, England—from which Arthur has banished him, praises the land in impas-

sioned words. I reproduce part of his soliloquy: "He! douce terre
pleinne de toutes beneürtez . . . beneoit soient tuit cil qui en toi
remanent, soient mi ami ou mi ennemi. . . . Victoire et honor lor doint
Dex . . . nus ne pourroit estre en si dolz païs com cist est qui ne fust
plus bien eürez que nus autres; por moi le di ge qui esprové l'ai"
(MA 123.1–12).

After quoting a somewhat smaller portion of the soliloquy, F. Lot
remarks that the words are comparable to those uttered by Mary Queen
of Scots on leaving France, but concludes that "nous ne sommes pas en
droit" to believe that the author was expressing his own sentiments,
since Lancelot has every reason to have such feelings regarding "la
Grande Bretagne" (LEt 142n1). Frappier, in his analysis of the same
passage finds in it particularly "un regret poignant du passé" (FEt 235).
Undoubtedly such regrets exist in Lancelot, but he could lament the
past without heaping praise upon the land that has been the scene of
his late misfortunes. His expression is territorial, not temporal. As to
Lot's remarks, one could argue that Lancelot might very well have
mixed feelings concerning Great Britain; but even if he had every
reason to praise the island, his words might never have been invented
if the author of the *Mort Artu* had not sympathized with them, particularly if the author had reason to doubt that praise of England
would be welcome to his readers. The liegemen of Philip Augustus or
Louis VIII were not likely to be so pro-English as to enjoy them. Thus,
either the public addressed was expected to share Lancelot's sentiments
or the author of the *Mort Artu* had such overflowing love for England
that he seized an opportunity for expressing it. Or both conditions
existed. I say England rather than Great Britain because after the
soliloquy the next words are, "Itex paroles dist Lancelos quant il parti
del roiaume de Logres" (MA 124.1–2). Lot, before invoking the parallel to "Marie Stuart," might have remembered that the detailed record
of the widowed queen's regrets had been preserved by the Sieur de
Brantôme, a Frenchman. Lot would probably have granted that, if we
knew nothing of Shakespeare except the passage on "this England"
spoken in *Richard II*, we should conclude at once that the speech was
the work of an Englishman or of someone with an intimate experience
of England. Nor do we doubt that anyone who speaks nostalgically of
Paris knows Paris. On the same basis we might also be prepared to
think that the man who put nostalgic words into Lancelot's mouth
had had some dealings with England-Logres.

If the author of the *Mort Artu* was expressing his own leanings

through Lancelot's soliloquy, it becomes most appropriate to investigate
how much knowledge of English geography he reveals. M. Frappier
says that his knowledge was quite superficial, no greater than that
which any slightly cultivated Frenchman might have had. He says
further: "Notre romancier commet d'ailleurs de grosses erreurs: il
croit par exemple que la plaine de Salisbury est toute proche de la mer.
Enfin aucune ligne de son oeuvre ne révèle une connaissance person-
nelle des sites et des paysages, la sensation des choses vues" (FEt 22).
He cites two exceptions in a note which concludes: "Mais l'auteur
pouvait connaître ces détails par ouï-dire ou par ses sources." His judgment is: "Il n'avait certainement jamais franchi la mer" (FEt 22). He
reiterates his opinion: "Le romancier connaissait fort mal la géographie
de l'Angleterre" (FEt 174). He allowed these statements to remain
unqualified in the second edition of his thesis in 1961, but in 1969 he
speaks thus of the author of the *Mort Artu*: "Il reste fort douteux à
mon avis qu'il ait jamais visité l'Angleterre, bien qu'aujourd'hui je sois
moins opposé qu'autrefois à cette conjecture" (FBS 1016). Marjorie
Fox speaks in words similar to Frappier's early pronouncements,
though less forcefully (Fo 41). F. Lot, convinced that the Cycle was
the work of one man, says: "L'auteur n'est ni Normand ni Anglo-
Normand . . . il sait ce qu'un Français continental instruit pouvait
connaître de son temps" (LEt 140); later he adds, "L'auteur de la
Mort d'Arthur . . . ignorait la géographie de l'Angleterre" (LEt 196n5).
The opinions which the romance evoked from such scholarly readers
contrast sharply with the impression made by Lancelot's farewell.

The *Mort Artu* names three cities in Britain which every reader
knows are part of England: Winchester, Dover, and London. The
romance also portrays action on Salisbury Plain. For Dover and London it mentions one feature each, the castle at Dover and the Tower of
London. Perhaps M. Frappier's "tout Français un peu cultivé" knew
that the chief citadel of London was called simply the Tower, but
perhaps too the number of Frenchmen who had never crossed the
Channel and who were familiar with this fact was not great. In any
case the author of the *Mort Artu* gives the impression that he had in
mind no isolated tower. Guenevere assembles within it two hundred
men (142.8), besides stocking it with "toutes les choses, qui a cors
d'onme puissent aidier ne valoir, que l'en pot trover el païs" (142.15–
17). When she left, she "fist conduire hors de la tor deus somiers
chargiez d'or et d'argent" (170.5–7). The pack animals may have been
brought in at the moment of loading, but there still had to be room to

accommodate them within the fortress. Since nothing had been said earlier about bringing in gold and silver, the supply is presumably already in the Tower; the author seems to have regarded the Tower as a treasure house. When Mordred sends his men against it, the defenders "les ocient e abatent contreval les fossez" (142.86); after the assault two hundred dead lay "es fossez." The moats seem to have been extensive; the writer apparently knew that ditching formed the outer defenses of the Tower of London, which is not perched on high rocks. Moats to protect the Tower were first built in 1190. In Henry III's time much construction of buildings secondary to the keep was taking place.

As for Dover, M. Frappier is sufficiently impressed to refer to the author's knowledge of "la position dominante du château de Douvres sur la mer" (FEt 22n2). In the romance the brief description of Dover is contained within these words: "Il arriverent souz le chastel de Douvre; et quant il furent arrivé et il orent des nes ostees leur armes, li rois fist savoir a ceus de Douvre qu'il ouvrissent la porte et le receüssent leanz; et cil si fisent a grant joie" (171.5–9). The first clause of the quotation indicates accurately the location of the castle on heights rising from the shore. The harbor is somewhat to the west. Arthur thus landed on the beach below the castle and then treated with the citizens in their town built around the harbor. The topography indicated, though sketchy, is accurate.

The news of the arrival at Dover of Arthur and his army is immediately carried to Mordred, still besieging Guenevere in the Tower of London. The word is, "Artus venoit sor elz a tot son pooir et seroit a Londres dedenz tiers jour" (168.58–59). The distance from the port to the capital is correctly implied in this statement. The author of the *Mort Artu* does not measure distances in miles or leagues (with one exception), but he frequently tells us, as in this case, how many days it takes to cover the distance between two places.

Instead of marching toward London, Arthur and his forces head west, and in three days reach the Salisbury Plain. These were long marches, but feasible, in detail, as follows: After the king quits the cortège bearing Gawain's body to Kamaalot, he returns to Dover for the rest of the day. "A l'endemain s'en parti et s'esmut a aler encontre Mordret . . . la nuit jut a l'entree d'une forest" (176.4–7). On the way west the area still known as the Weald offers appropriate forest lands. That night Arthur has warnings from Gawain in a dream. His second day's march is leisurely because "il ne savoit de quele ore il enconterroit les gens Mordret" (176.48–50). They are, then, as they proceed west-ward, at the point nearest London on their march and might expect harassment from the forces gathered there.

At the end of this second day the halt is on "la praerie de Lovedon" (176.54–55). This stretch of meadowland should be at a point between one-half and two-thirds of the distance from Dover to Salisbury Plain. For the moment, geographical nomenclature is not so important as the fact that at an appropriate point between Dover and Salisbury Plain there is a meadow large enough for the bivouac of a large force. Such a meadow exists. About four miles northeast of Basingstoke the upper waters of the river Lodden flow through lands so flat that the Lodden and the Lyde pursue a closely parallel course for miles, with only flat bottom between them. In Arthur's sleep that night comes the apparition of Fortune and her wheel that expresses an underlying idea of the romance.

The next day, "chevalcha li rois vers les plains de Salesbieres au plus droit que il pot onques, comme cil qui bien savoit que en cele plaigne seroit la grant bataille mortex dont Merlins et li autre devineor avoient assez parlé" (178.1–5). Before nightfall he is on the plain. From the beginning the prophecies have evidently determined not only Arthur's movements but those of Mordred also. From London the usurper also heads straight for the plain.

The author of the *Mort Artu* knew more about the Salisbury Plain than its location. After Arthur's arrival on it, "celui soir aprés souper s'ala li rois Artus esbatre aval la plaigne entre lui et l'arcevesque, et tant qu'il vindrent a une roche haute et dure" (178.10–13). The rock bears an inscription made long years before, "lonc tens a," saying that a fatal battle is to take place on a site near there. Merlin had caused it to be chiseled. Archeological inscriptions are not characteristic of the area, but "roches hautes et dures" are. M. Frappier calls this passage from the *Mort Artu* "une réminiscence des pierres géantes, des trilites de Stonehenge" (FEt 176n7), and again a "souvenir assez vague des trilithes de Stonehenge" (FEt 22n2). The passage might be consid-ered somewhat vague if only trilithons, erected stones capped by a lintel, were to be found at Stonehenge; but it becomes more precise when we remember that there are monoliths, especially the Heelstone. In the general region, especially at Avesbury, one may also inspect monoliths standing in isolation.

We have already seen that M. Frappier has stated that the author of the *Mort Artu* could have known little of England's geography because he places Salisbury Plain near the sea. M. Fox finds too that "il situe la plaine de Salisbury trop près de la mer" (Fo 41). F. Lot, with a bit of reasoning, had already made a similar affirmation: The author "s'imaginait . . . que cette localité n'est pas très éloignée de la mer puisque Arthur, mortellement blessé, peut, quittant le champ de bataille de 'Salesbières' gagner, à cheval il est vrai, le rivage de la mer" (LEt 196*n*5).

The basis of these comments is in the following passage: "Lors monte seur un cheval assez legierement; il se partent del chanp en tel maniere tuit troi et errent droit vers la mer, tant qu'il vindrent a une chapele qui avoit non la Noire Chapele" (191.27–31). Later we learn that the Black Chapel is half a day's journey from the sea. The ride from the battlefield is *toward* not *to* the sea. (The context here makes it impossible to accept "aler vers" in the terminating sense that Modern French "aller vers" often has.) The Chapel itself was not near the battlefield; such is the implication of the lines quoted—particularly the verb "errent," which contains the notion of continuous riding. Lot is reasonable when he says that a battle-weary and mortally wounded man would seem unfitted for a long ride. The *Mort Artu*, however, insists upon Arthur's vigor up to the moment when the king confides Excalibur to Girflet. We have seen that he mounts his horse "assez legierement"; at the chapel he prays till morning, and then he crushes Lucan to death in his embrace; leaving the chapel, he rides afterward for hours, from early morning till "eure de midi" (192.27), to reach the seashore. Salisbury Plain is, then, for the author of the *Mort Artu*, not very near the sea, probably no closer than it actually is. And the sea is as close to the west as to the south.

The entombment of Arthur in the Black Chapel, an element not found in the works of Geoffrey or Wace, is not necessary to the romance, and detracts from the mystery of the departure by sea. The episode must have been inserted into the *Mort Artu* because readers of the time expected an account of the king's ending to leave his body where the whole world knew it rested.

The Black Chapel, M. Frappier and others to the contrary, was located where Glastonbury is. In view of the superhuman strength of the stricken king, an evening and night ride from Salisbury Plain to Glastonbury was no impossible matter, for, as Malory says of the distance from Amesbury to Glastonbury, it "is lytel more than thirty myle" (Vin1255.27). Glastonbury is about fifteen miles from the sea, a proper distance for the ride of Arthur and Girflet from the Black

Chapel. By the time the *Mort Artu* was written, it was common knowledge that Arthur's body had been found at Glastonbury. To make the location acceptable, we do not have to assume that instead of "N" we should have "V" at the beginning of "Noire Chapele." Certain manuscripts write "V," but the substitution, if such it is, means nothing more than that the scribe who made it thought that he must be seeing that letter in the original because, if you talk of Glastonbury, you must talk of glass: such an idea was not new. Let us grant that the earliest manuscript had "N": the explanation as to why "black" should have been used to identify the chapel seems simple. Glastonbury was an establishment of Benedictines, "black monks"; "black," then, serves to suggest Glastonbury without saying so in outright terms. The author of the *Mort Artu* knew that the "white abbeys" of the *Queste* are a key to the Cistercian connections of that romance. In any case, the Black Chapel, as the place of Arthur's interment, would have had to stand on the site of Glastonbury.

The account in the Margan Annals (R36 I.21) reports that people say ("dicunt") that a second man's bones found in the tomb with Arthur were those of Mordred. The author of the *Mort Artu* could hardly tolerate such a combination, and would desire to provide another identity for the second male skeleton. Thus we may explain the death of Lucan the Butler from Arthur's embrace and the burial of sovereign and vassal side by side before the chapel's altar. The Black Chapel was of course not the later church of Glastonbury Abbey; by calling it a chapel the author was telling his readers that they should understand that the small, old building had fallen into ruins and been replaced in later centuries.

Even the lake into which Excalibur was thrown had its parallel in the country near the sea to the west of Glastonbury. The marshes by the river Brue are usually drained now, but earlier allowed Glastonbury to be called an island. A pool in those marshes could have received Excalibur.

The author of the *Mort Artu* displays knowledge of southern England, and might indeed have been well acquainted with it. Apparently, on the other hand, he had little acquaintance with the north—the farther north, the less. The Castle of Joyous Guard on the River Humber is the refuge of Lancelot and Guenevere after her rescue from death by burning at the stake. In this case the *Mort Artu* contains no allusions that allow us to measure distances. Nothing shows that the author knew this region personally or through good informants; he had inherited the Humber location from the *Galehaut* but could not describe the country.

One part of the Welsh border seems to have been within his knowledge. The second tournament chronicled in the *Mort Artu* takes place at Tanebourc, which was "uns chastiaus moult forz et moult bien sëanz a l'entree de Norgales" (25.11–12). As we shall see later, the *Mort Artu* also locates it at nine days' ride, with stops, from a spot rather near London; the number of days seems reasonable for the trip to the north Welsh border. We can agree with Lot that Tanebourc is a name derived from Tenebroc in Chrestien's *Erec*. It seems, however, to replace a real name; the other tournaments in the *Mort Artu* are held at well-known towns, Winchester and Kamaalot. Oswestry may well be meant; it was strong and well situated. Near Tanebourc the king of North Wales has a "recet" (37.19), perhaps an allusion to the castle of Dinas Bran twelve miles north-northwest of Oswestry. Between the two lies Chirk Castle, also famous and squarely on the border. If the "recet" was on the site of Dinas Bran, then Tanebourc may best be considered on the site of Chirk. If the "recet" can be located where Chirk is, then Tanebourc stood where Oswestry stands.

The *Mort Artu* contains two statements about the distance from Winchester to Tanebourc. A squire sees Lancelot where the latter lies ill just outside of Winchester and tells him in the evening, "Ge vois a Taneborc ou li tornoiemenz devoit estre et sera d'ui en tierz jor" (40.4–6). The squire leaves the next morning, and at the castle of the king of North Wales near Tanebourc on the evening before the tournament tells Gawain concerning Lancelot, "Je me parti de lui ier matin" (41.121). Thus the squire took two days to ride from Winchester to Tanebourc. It is 150 air miles from Winchester to Oswestry. The squire was young and traveling alone with light equipment, but still the journey ascribed to him is very long for only two days. The author of the *Mort Artu* or his informant might have thought the journey feasible for a young fellow; but it may be that the author or informant was acquainted with other roads to the North Welsh border better than with that from Winchester, and did not quite know the length of the stint set for the squire. In any case the distances implied are too nearly correct to be aught but the result of an effort at realism.[1]

---

[1] Montgomery is the only border fortress farther south in North Wales to merit consideration as the site of Tanebourc. Choosing it would reduce the distance from Winchester by twenty miles, but its neighborhood must be eliminated from discussion

Places mentioned as being situated near Tanebourc are Athean (37.16) and Tauroc (48.3-4). Athean is said to be eight leagues from the "recet" of the king of North Wales; it is also a day's journey distant from Tanebourc—an easy day's journey. Possibly the author had in mind the place designated in modern topography as High Hatton, some twenty miles east of Oswestry. (Hatton and Athean have some resemblances in sound.)[2] As for Tauroc (Sommer has a variant, Tanroc, and probably the handwriting could be so interpreted in several manuscripts), it too is at a day's journey from Tanebourc—toward London, and therefore to the southeast. For it there is a possibility in Tong Knoll. A knoll does not usually suggest a rock to speakers of English, but the steepness of Tong Knoll is such that it was chosen to be surmounted by a tower, as shown on the maps of the Ordnance Survey. I do not insist on the correctness of these identifications. It is, however, clear that the *Mort Artu* is quite specific about locations near Tanebourc; this quasi-precision, contrasted with its silence in regard to the country near Joyous Guard, suggests that it is dealing with an area of which he had some knowledge, directly or indirectly acquired.

Winchester is the scene of action near the end of the *Mort Artu*. There nothing appears to establish spatial relationships between it and other places. But Bohort finds it a fitting place to bury his brother Lionel "com l'en dut fere cors de roi" (201.9), an allusion to other royal entombments there. The tournament at Winchester in the early part of the *Mort Artu* takes place on its "praerie" (16.67). King Arthur and his party stationed themselves on "la plus mestre tor de la vile por veoir le tornoiement" (17.2-3). The terminology "de la vile" implies that the king is not in his own castle but on the city's fortifications. Beyond the east gate, protected by towers, lie the grounds that once held the famous fair flourishing under the Normans. The river Itchen flows beside them. Before the establishment of the fair, the grounds should have been ideal for tourneying. Even though other towns present similar arrangements, the author has said nothing inconsistent with the character of Winchester.

---

because Montgomery is definitely over the border on the Welsh side. There was no English fortress corresponding to it, like Oswestry or a borderline stronghold like Chirk; that is, there was no provision for both a center at Tanebourc and a neighboring castle for the king of North Wales.

[2] A phonemic transcription of the two names as probably pronounced by a Frenchman of the thirteenth century shows that only the second vowel element is different: Hatton/atõn/ ; Athean/ateãn/.

At the beginning of the *Mort Artu* we learn that Winchester is at a rather easy two days' journey from Kamaalot. Through this circumstance and some others it becomes possible to place where Kamaalot lay in the mind of the author, which is not to say that most romances had the same location for the fabled city. They may have placed it in the air or in a region far away from that demonstrably chosen by the author of the *Mort Artu*; for him it was definitely situated. Almost always people have thought of it as being well to the west of Winchester. In the *Mort Artu* it is not only two days' journey from that city; it is also at the same distance from Dover. It took two days to transport Gawain's body from the seaport to its resting place in the church of St. Stephen at Kamaalot. Two days from Winchester, two days from Dover; the circles described at the proper distances from these two places intersect in the English Channel and somewhere near London, hardly farther north, for the distances become too great.

Kamaalot of the *Mort Artu* was on the banks of a major river. The circumstances surrounding the arrival of the boat bearing the dead maid of Escalot make such a stream necessary. There is evidently an important landing stage "desoz la tour a Kamaalot" (70.3) where the boat docks. Not only can Arthur and Gawain come down to examine the vessel's content, but also "li haut home furent descendu del palés et venu au pié de la tour pour veoir qu'il avoit en la nacele" (71.48–50). Between the Thames and the English Channel there is no stream of such proportions. Kamaalot must then be on the Thames near London. London itself is not meant, for we have seen that in that city much action near the end of the romance takes place. There is no action that goes from one town to the other. Kamaalot is the scene whenever we are concerned with the personal life of the court; London, with political life. But still we must be near London, and nothing in the story makes nearness impossible.

If we undertake to determine which of the towns near medieval London can be identified with Kamaalot, we must find one where there was a royal palace close beside the river. Despite the temptation to think that quite a number of miles must separate the two capitals, our choice must fall upon Westminster. Westminster was a favorite scene of activity for the English kings from the reign of William II well past the time of the composition of the *Mort Artu*. For Englishmen in Angevin times, Westminster and London were distinct entities, as separate from each other as Vincennes from Paris for the subjects of Louis IX—or, to cite a more familiar though later parallel, Versailles from Paris. Westminster Palace was next to the river, possessed a quay of its own, and offered the king a view of the waters, as the following excerpts from the Close Rolls of the years 1236 and 1238 show:

> Mandatum est Odoni aurifabro quod reparari faciat kayum regis apud Westmonasterium quod nuper confractum est per inundationem aquarum; faciat etiam fieri oriolum quod est inter novam cameram regis et receptam versus Tamisiam, sicut rex ei precepit cum esset apud Lond. (Year 1236, ClR III.245)

> Mandatum est custodibus operationum suarum de Westmonasterio quod archeam subtus privatam cameram regis versus aquam Tamisie bonis et fortibus barris ferreis barrari faciat. (Year 1238, ClR IV.99)

The "mestre eglise" of Kamaalot is St. Stephen's. There Gaheris, the victim of the poisoned apple, the maid of Escalot, and the lady of Beloe are buried; there Gawain and his brothers are put to rest; there Lancelot directed that his shield shall hang, "si que tuit cil qui des ore mes le verront aient en remenbrance les merveilles que ge ai fetes en ceste terre" (120.17–19). The author's predilection for this church impresses M. Frappier, and he hazards the guess that the author of the *Mort Artu* was connected with St. Stephen's at Meaux. Without denying this possibility, we may still attach significance to the fact that at Westminster also there was a St. Stephen's. The chapel royal of Westminster Palace was consecrated to that saint. By saying of the "Mostier Saint Estiene" that "*alors* estoit la mestre iglise de Kamaalot" (102.9) the author of the *Mort Artu* acknowledged that by his time, as contrasted with "alors," another church had gained the ascendancy. But in his time St. Stephen's was still prominent. In 1226 the Close Rolls record that William "de Castellis" was to be paid five marks "ad vestimenta et quendam calicem emenda ad capellam nostram Sancti Stephani de Westm" (ClR II.117). The following passages from the Close Rolls are of more interest:

> Mandatum est H. de Path', thesaurio, quod de marmore, quem (sic) habet penes se et qui (sic) debuit retineri ad opus Thome de Muleton, fieri faciat decentes gradus ante altare in capella Sancti Stephani apud Westmonasterium et de residuo ejusdem Marmoris faciat gradus ante altare in capella regine apud Westmonasterium ex quo perfecta fuerit; et si marmor ille (sic) non sufficiat ad

utrumque opus tunc de tegula picta gradus illos fieri faciat; parvam etiam capellam apud Westmonasteruim tegula picta decenter paveari faciatis (sic) et a tergo ultra sedem regis in eadem capella faciat depingi historiam Joseph. (Year 1238, ClR IV.26)

Mandatum est H. de Pateshull, thesaurio domini regis, quod borduram a tergo sedis regis in capella Sancti Stephani apud Westmonasterium et borduram a tergo sedis regine ex alia parte ejusdem capelle internis et externis depingi faciat de viridi colore; juxta sedem ipsius regine depingi faciat quandam crucem cum Maria et Johanne ex opposito crucis regis que juxta sedem regis depicta est. (Year 1236, ClR III.239)

The final building of St. Stephen's Chapel has been attributed to Edward I. Because Parliament sat in St. Stephen's for centuries, its name became a synonym of parliament. Of course the author of the *Mort Artu* foresaw none of these later developments. But he could well have known St. Stephen's as a place frequented by many people of gentle birth. The Curia Regis Rolls for 1227 have an account of a conference or conversation concerning a heritage that took place "in capella Sancti Stephani apud Westmonasterium" (CRR XIII.83). The participants were small gentry. This evidence of quasi-public use and the references cited above to smaller chapels in the royal palace (Henry III's sister was married in one; R57 III.470) help justify the *Mort Artu*'s transformation of the pretentious royal chapel of Westminster Palace into the "mestre eglise" of Kamaalot. Replacing the name Westminster with Kamaalot is understandable even without alleging that Arthur lived before the name Westminster with its Germanic element had come into being; the favorite capital of King Arthur could bear no other name than Kamaalot.

The quotations from the Close Rolls reveal that the walls of St. Stephen's at Westminster were decorated with paintings. In the *Agravain* one motif utilizes wall paintings in St. Stephen's at Kamaalot. Lancelot, traveling with Mordred, hears a "prudhomme," who is killed for his pains, prophesy to the incestuous son that he will destroy his father; he says that Arthur is cognizant of this future event and has caused a serpent to be painted on the walls of St. Stephen's at Kamaalot to remind him of the prospect (V.284.32). Later, in the presence of King Arthur, Lancelot sees the serpent on the church walls during a ceremony. The source of this prophetic use of painting is in this case, it seems, a story similar to one that Giraldus Cambrensis tells of Henry II. Gerald recorded in *De Principis Instructione* that on the walls of the palace of Winchester Henry had painted an eagle being torn by the beaks and claws of his eaglets. He explained to his "familiaribus," well before his family attacked him in 1173, that the eagle stood for him and the eaglets for his sons, who would revolt against him and tear his dominions apart (R21 VIII.295). Gerald's tale is evidently related to the myth of the pelican offering as food to its young the flesh of its own breast. The motivation of the parent has disappeared in Gerald's version; that of the progeny is somewhat altered. In the *Agravain* there is no longer any resemblance to the legend of the pelican, but the essential of Gerald's story remains: a king causes to be painted on the walls of a building which he frequents a reminder of a future calamity to be brought on him by his male progeny. In both versions an explanation takes place in a company that includes one of the principals and a third party who reflects upon it later. For our present purposes the most significant element in the version of the tale presented in the *Agravain* is that its wall paintings are located in St. Stephen's at Kamaalot. The same real sanctuary may well have inspired both the *Agravain* and the *Mort Artu*.

Malory locates Camelot at Winchester (Vin 1065.4); but incidents which the *Mort Artu* sets at Kamaalot, he places at Westminster. That is, the victim of the poisoned apple is buried at Westminster (Vin 1059.26–27), and the dead maid of Astolat is given a boatman who "stirred the large bargett unto Westmynster" (Vin 1095.12).[3]

In the *Mort Artu*, the funeral party conveying Gawain's body from Dover to Kamaalot stops the first night at the castle of Beloé or Beloe (174.3), where a husband kills his wife for lamenting Gawain as a lost

---

[3] It is probable that all authors of the pseudo-Map Cycle thought of Kamaalot as located on the site of Westminster. In Volume III the reference to the distance from Flodehueg to Kamaalot, in conjunction with the evidence from the *Mort Artu*, implies that Kamaalot was near London. In Volume IV the reference to Camaalot, "de Logres la cité" four days from Carduel (cited at the beginning of Chapter III), implies as much. The reference to St. Stephen's in the *Agravain* (V.284.32) seems very strong evidence that the author had Henry III's royal chapel at Westminster in mind.

Apropos of the voyage of the dead maid of Astolat, G. R. Stewart remarks, "Malory has in this manner transformed the voyage of a magical boat into an entirely realistic occurrence" (St 206). If we compare the *Mort Artu* version of the last trip of the maid of Escalot with the voyagings of Percival's sister in the *Queste*, the source often cited (for instance, BE I.427; FEt 212–14), we see that the episode in the *Mort Artu* is less "magical" than the one in the *Queste*. Malory has managed some increase in realism, mainly by making outright statements on geography instead of limiting himself to hints. See further note 4, below.

love. In this area one day out from Dover toward London, place-names with any resemblance to Beloe are not widespread, but several occur close together. Eight miles northeast of Tunbridge Wells is the village of Beltring, with Beltring House close beside it. A mile or so to the east flows the river Beult, and on its bank is Benover. As in the case of the secondary places near Tanebourc, the author of the *Mort Artu* has attached a name to a spot at a day's ride from a major place. I am no more sure that Beloe has a relationship to the above-cited names in "Bel" than I am that the "Ath" of Athean is akin to the "Hat" of Hatton or the "Tan" of Tanroc to the "Ton" of Tong Knoll. If there are such relations, it is to be observed that in adapting all these names, the *Mort Artu* is rather faithful to the beginning of the word and made alterations for the end. The same phenomenon is visible in two additional cases of names for spots also one day's ride from major places. In at least one of these cases, Escalot, there is more cogent evidence to aid in identification.

Of Escalot, F. Lot exclaims: "L'auteur n'a aucune idée de la situa-tion de cette localité; pour lui elle est quelque part du côté de Win-chester!" Lot is so emphatic because he is sure that Escalot is in Scot-land. Citing as substantiation page 269 of Bruce's edition of the *Mort Artu*, he arrives at that conclusion by etymologizing: "*Escalot* ou *Ascalot* est certainement une déformation de *Ascelud, Acelud* [in Geoffrey] . . . cacographie pour Aclut (Dumbarton sur la Clyde)" (LEt 143*n*16). Even if the etymon is correctly determined, we may wonder why Lot considers that the author of the *Mort Artu* shows ignorance of British geography in placing his Escalot wherever he liked.

At the beginning of the *Mort Artu*, to go secretly to Winchester for the tournament "si tost comme il furent communalment couchié par la cité de Kamaalot" (9.1–3), Lancelot and his squire quit Kamaa-lot. "Il se furent mis el droit chemin a aler a Wincestre, il chevauchie-rent toute la nuit en tel maniere que onques ne se reposerent. L'en-demain, quant il fu jorz, vindrent a un chastel ou li rois avoit jeü la nuit" (9.13–10.2). The castle is at Escalot (see particularly 25.15). Lancelot puts up with a "vavasor," father of the "damoisele d'Escalot" (first complete occurrence of the name, 71.9), father also of two newly made knights qualified as "freres del chastel d'Escalot" (18.25). The vavasor lives outside the main castle, "forteresce" (25.16), where the king has lain, but his family is regularly referred to as being of the "chastel d'Escalot." Lancelot stays here through the day. "Quant il fu anuitié, si s'en parti de chiés le vavasor . . . Toute nuit chevaucha . . . tant qu'il vindrent l'endemain un pou ainz le soleil levant a une liue de Wincestre" (15.2–8). The castle is on the "droit chemin" from Kamaalot to Winchester. It is also on a stream flowing down past Kamaalot broad enough to convey the "nacelle" of the dead maid.

Even if we did not already know that Escalot, in order to be on the way from Kamaalot to the scene of the tournament, must be northeast of Winchester, we should arrive at the same conclusion from its topographical characteristics combined only with the knowledge of its distance from Winchester. On a circle drawn at the distance of a night's ride from that city we find no suitable stream except to the northeast; to the south the circle runs through the sea, in most other directions through hill country. To the northeast it intersects the valley of the river Wey approximately at Guildford. The topographical characteristics of Guildford fit well the description of Escalot to be deduced from the *Mort Artu*. The river Wey is in this part of its course so broad and placid that boating is a main amusement, and boats reach the size of launches. The castle stands on a steep knob extending out from a higher hill beyond. The road from London comes down the High Street, and that street is so close to the castle keep that underground crypts below the roadway are traditionally regarded as being part of the castle structure. The romance tells us that King Arthur at a window, lifting his head, recognizes Lancelot as he approaches at the "trespas d'une rue" (11.5). He could easily have done so if Lancelot were riding down what has become High Street into the village clustered by the river. The king expects to catch sight of Lancelot after he has passed beyond the castle, as he might well have done if the knight had not "el chastel . . . entrez en une meson" (11.14–16). The castle is here understood as enclosing within it at least part of the town. The house is that of the vavasor of Escalot. King Arthur is evidently in his own royal possession; the vavasor is not the lord of the castle, simply the inhabitant of a "meson." Later in the romance we divine that the "meson" is not small; behind it is a considerable garden, a "prael" (26.2). Gawain and his brothers lodge at this house. Their host and his daughter invite them into the "prael," where Gawain is able to have a tête-à-tête with the maiden because "Gaheriez trest l'oste en sus" (26.9), and "Mordrés se fu tret en sus" (26.12). Though "en sus" may mean nothing more than "away," the insistence upon the term implies that the author was speaking of a garden on a hillside, just as would be the case if the "meson" were by Guildford Castle.

We may infer that directly or indirectly the author of the *Mort Artu* was acquainted with Guildford, which would not be surprising in a man interested in Winchester and Westminster. Guildford was a "royal castle," the king's possession (BoH 176). Henry II was there 13 August 1179 (BoH 557). In December, 1184, after reconciling his sons at Windsor in the presence of their mother, the *Gesta Henrici* says that the king proceeded to Guildford and there gave Richard permission to return to Poitou (R49 I.334). Presumably Eleanor was still with him then. The king kept Christmas there (25–26 December) in 1186, though, ever on the move, he was in Westminster by the first of January (Sa 250). John kept Easter at Guildford in 1205, and was there again 27–28 December 1207 and 25–27 January 1208 (ClR I.26, 99, 101). Henry III resided there quite often. The Liberate Rolls contain numerous directives for wine to be delivered at Guildford; in 1227, 1237, and 1240 there were orders for building construction (LR I, summarized in SU III.557–58). The operations of 1251 were extensive (R27 II.66). Many royal documents were issued from the town. Henry stayed there for days at a time as he went from Windsor or Westminster or reversed his path; the Liberate Rolls show that he was there at least twelve times, including Pentecost 1228 and Easter 1229 (LR I). In May and June, 1228, he stopped first on his way from Westminster to Winchester, then again as he went back to Windsor. In July, 1238, he was there on his way from Winchester to Westminster. Thus, in the early thirteenth century for a king to stop at his castle at Guildford was common as he progressed from the palaces on the Thames to Winchester. Malory says that the tournament to which Arthur and Lancelot are riding is at Camelot, but since he locates Camelot at Winchester, he and the *Mort Artu* name the same destination. For Malory the point of departure is London. After a day's journey "the kynge lodged at a town that was called Astolat, that ys in English Gylforde" (Vin 1065.27). By equating Astolat and Guildford he was likely following a tradition, though he may have arrived at the identification by processes similar to those set forth above. If the latter case, he proves that another man has reasoned as I have; if the former, that people early recognized Guildford in Escalot.[4]

---

[4] Vinaver comments, "M's identification of Astolat with Guildford, roughly a day's journey from London, makes it seem natural that Arthur on his way to Winchester should break his journey at Astolat" (Vin 1601). So it does, and so thought the author of the *Mort Artu*, I doubt not. Vinaver remarks often on Malory's rationalizing tendency.

It would be difficult to explain what relation the name "Astolat" has to Guildford; it is easy to find the connection in the case of "Escalot." Beside Guildford is Shalford. The village is not two miles away, and Shalford Park lies against Guildford about one-half mile from the castle. In thirteenth-century records Latinized examples of Shalford, this Shalford, beginning with "Sca" occur (Year 1211, CRR VI.130; Year 1221, P I.497; Year 1275, Ipm II.96, item 153; Year 1265, Imc I.273, item 902). A speaker of a Romance language would naturally alter "Sca" to "Esca"; the termination "ot" instead of a translation of "ford" seems to be an analogy with the ending of Kamaalot, supposedly arrived at from "Camelford."[5] Besides, since in the Latinized versions of the names of English towns the termination describing topography or function may be replaced, as in the cases of Glastonbury, Worcester, and Oxford, the author of the *Mort Artu* would feel at liberty to follow his fancy in gallicizing Shalford.

In speaking of Tanebourc I said that it was nine days' meandering ride from a point near London; that point is Escalot. Lancelot's kindred spend eight days searching for him after leaving Escalot (37.9), and then halt at Athean one day out from Tanebourc (37.16). For the return ride a corresponding period elapses. After the tournament

---

Others have observed a similar tendency in the *Mort Artu*. Frappier says, "Les chevaliers ne peuvent plus s'égarer dans la féerie; ils sont constraints à la réalité la plus dramatique, celle de l'homme et de sa destinée" (FEt 292). Bruce speaks of the author's "sparing use of the supernatural" (BE I.434). Lot comments more drastically upon his supposed single author of the Cycle, "L'auteur a une tournure d'esprit tout à fait evhémériste. . . Le malheureux ne croit même pas aux fées . . . les êtres surnaturels sont transformés en personnages du XIII° siècle" (LEt 272–23). Specifically of the *Mort Artu* he declares, "Par crainte du surnaturel l'auteur finit par se résigner à laisser mourir et enterrer Arthur" (LEt 273n5). As in the case commented upon in note 3, Malory was carrying on a tendency already existent. The author of the *Mort Artu* did not identify Escalot quite by name. He left a mild puzzle for those contemporary readers to whom Winchester was a feature of a known land.

Vinaver quotes G. R. Stewart, "In Malory's time the residential portions of Guildford Castle were already in a ruinous condition [Stewart cites G. C. Williamson, *Guildford Castle*, Guildford, 1926; the ultimate source is the Liberate Rolls, probably via *The Victoria History of Surrey*], and for that reason could probably be all the more readily associated with the ancient times of Arthur" (St 206). Few would know about a dilapidated building not visited by the king; many would be acquainted with a castle and palace of the thirteenth century where the court often stopped and building was going on.

[5] In view of circumstances to be developed later it is interesting that the son of the first William Longsword, who bore his father's full name, through marriage with Idonea de Camvil became lord of (among other manors) Shalford Manor about 1226 (Su III.108).

Gawain joins Bohort and company in searching for Lancelot. The quest brings them back to Escalot. Gawain says to his host there, "L'avons quis plus de uit jorz" (44.84).

Let us consider again the possible relationship between Lovedon and Lodden. Lovedon meant much to the author of the *Mort Artu* as the place where Arthur has the dream that shows him Fortune's wheel, an important thematic system for him and his contemporaries. He takes the trouble to give the spot a name, whereas the setting of the dream visit of Gawain the night before remains anonymous. Transforming Lodden into Lovedon would be in harmony with a technique already discussed. This time, however, the altered name is that borne with the same spelling by other places in England; there were Lovedons in Essex (Ipm I.23, item 100) and in Lincolnshire (Ipm II.423, item 689). If the author of the *Mort Artu* replaces Lodden by a similar name borrowed from another locality, he is following the same procedure which appears to have been used by the author of the *Benoic-Gaunes* in replacing Bron by Brion and Guesnes by Gaunes.

Though there are in the preceding pages on the *Mort Artu* a few English place identifications which I, probably in much company, consider problematical, the places most important for the story are those for which the exactness of location is surest. The features of the Black Chapel country correspond well to those of the Glastonbury region. Kamaalot as Westminster and Escalot as Shalford-Guildford are to my mind identifications firmly established. The author of the *Mort Artu* should be cleared of the charge of ignorance of the land where the action of his romance takes place.

The procedures of the authors of the *Mort Artu* and the *Benoic-Gaunes* in handling toponyms are remarkably similar. Both employ the usual names for certain locations: the Loire and Bourges in the *Benoic-Gaunes*; Dover, Winchester, London, and Salisbury Plain in the *Mort Artu*. Both use somewhat disguised names to replace the real in referring to the scene of events in small population centers; Trebes-Trèves, Shalford-Escalot. Both replace the names of capitals by unrelated names—Saumur-Benoic, Westminster-Kamaalot—but leave traces to permit identification by those curious about, or acquainted with, the capitals, the castle of Haut Mur, and St. Stephen's Chapel.

The pronounced tendency to spatial realism in the *Mort Artu* is accompanied by realistic allocations of time. Since time and space are so important to the author of the *Mort Artu*, we may expect him to

5 ❦ Historical Background of the Mort Artu

ertain historical implications are allied to the foregoing observations on topography. I shall make no concerted effort to search out historical reminiscences in the part of the *Mort Artu* preceding the campaigns of King Arthur against Lancelot, though there are even in the early part of the romance traces of connections between it and history to which I may incidentally call attention.

The first feature of the *Mort Artu* forcibly to strike the reader as influenced by the events of the late twelfth and early thirteenth century is the successful interference of the pope in King Arthur's marital affairs, also utilized in the *False Guenevere*. Because the pope had triumphed over Henry II and his son John, and had forced Philip II to take back a wife whom he had put away, similar success with Arthur is credible. It would be foolish to say that Arthur resembles Philip or that Ingeborg was like Guenevere, but the influence of recent history on the romance is clear. That fact suggests that other reminiscences of thirteenth-century history are to be found in it.

Tactically it seems strange that, on returning home to fight Mordred, Arthur should land at Dover and then march straight to Salisbury Plain. To be sure, in the *Historia Regum Britanniae* Arthur lands at Richborough, as far east as Dover, and fights his last battle in Cornwall; but, like William the Conqueror, he finds enemies attacking his forces as he lands. His march west is a pursuit. In the *Mort Artu* there is no resistance at Dover; Arthur is not in pursuit of the enemy as he heads west. It also seems strange that Mordred, instead of seeking battle elsewhere, should follow a route parallel to Arthur's from London to the plain. It might perhaps be a sufficient explanation that the author portrays the battle as fated to take place where it does, but the tactics must have seemed more credible to thirteenth-century readers because combatants in England had recently acted similarly. When Philip Augustus's son Louis invaded England, his forces landed at Sandwich and proceeded to the capture of London. John, not daring to face him, looked at his fleet and rode to Dover. Thence he fled westward to Winchester and, after a pause, still farther into the western counties, heading first toward Corfe Castle and ending at Gloucester. He evidently passed through or close to the Salisbury Plain and through or close to Glastonbury. Louis left London along the route that we have already traced for Mordred, taking Reigate, Guildford, Odeham, and Farnham and proceeded on the way to Winchester, which he also captured. Salisbury soon surrendered to him. The parallel between the fictional marches of the sixth century and those of 1216 is obviously close.

A proper name late in the *Mort Artu* may serve as an entering wedge for studying parallels between individual actors in romance and history. Lancelot in his last battle, that at Winchester, comes upon "le conte de Gorre, qu'il connoist a traïtor et a desloial" (198.29–30). The count flees, but after a long pursuit (which results in Lancelot's being lost) Lancelot kills him. Gorre is celebrated in romance chiefly as the realm of Baudemagus the noble and Meleagant the traitorous, created in Chrétien's *Charrette*. Though it is possible that the name Gorre was evoked in the mind of the author of the *Mort Artu* by the recollection of Meleagant, the possibility is unlikely because Meleagant has already been recalled by the name Melehan assigned to the elder of Mordred's sons (197.29), who kills Lionel. Rather, whatever Gorre may have meant to Chrétien or his antecedents or modern scholars, the name is so similar to that of Gower that a public familiar with the names Salisbury and Winchester would associate the name with the district in southwest Wales. Thus, it seems that the author is arranging for Lancelot to take vengeance on a Welsh antagonist. The troubles of the earls of Pembroke with their neighbors, particularly LLewellyn, were interminable. And the earl of Pembroke from 1189 till 1219 was William Marshal; his sons succeeded him. Lancelot is thus acting as William would sometimes have liked to act.

There is no parallel to be drawn between most of Lancelot's adulterous career and that of William Marshal; there is, however, a perceptible similarity between the two men after Lancelot has renounced love as a director of behavior. King Arthur wages war against Lancelot for carrying off and defending Queen Guenevere. Pushed by

Gawain the king continues to be a persecutor of the hero nearly till his own death, attacking his former friend in Benoic and Gaunes. In his hour of need the king refuses to call upon Lancelot, convinced, he says (166.29–31), that a man whom he now recognizes as greatly wronged would never heed his plea. After Arthur's death, however, fidelity brings the old knight of the Round Table back from overseas to defeat the usurping sons of Mordred.

King John, particularly in the years 1208–1212, made life as miserable as possible for William Marshal, who had been one of his steadiest adherents from the beginning. During this period William was often in his Irish domains, where he was nearly sovereign. John went there in 1210. At Dublin before his court the king attacked his vassal, primarily because he had harbored a fugitive, William de Braose:

> Lors encoupa le marechal
> De mainz griés dunt grevé l'eüst
> Molt volentiers se le peüst. (GM 14286–88)

The court supported William. When the barons rose against John two years before his death, Marshal, in spite of the king's past conduct, remained faithful to him. John on his deathbed said:

> Por Dieu, preiez le marechal
> Qu'il me pardoinge les sorfeiz
> E les mals qu'a tort le ai faiz
>
> . . . .
>
> Vos pri qu'il ait mon fiz en garde
> E que toz dis s'en tient e garde. (GM 15174–88)

Marshal became the regent and successful defender of the young Henry III against Louis, the French invader.

The common character of these two recitals can be stated thus: The monarch of Britain becomes an enemy of a virtuous and faithful knight, long his friend. He pursues him overseas for harboring a fugitive who has incurred his displeasure, and displays vindictiveness there. He finally sees that he is in error. The noble knight persists in his fidelity and delivers Great Britain after the king's death from a usurping element. To those who say that Constantine's defeat of Mordred's sons in Geoffrey's *Historia Regum Britanniae* provides the sole source for the end of the *Mort Artu*, it may be observed that Constantine is advancing his own fortunes, while Lancelot, like Marshal, comes only as an avenger of his sovereign without interested motives. Also Lancelot, like Marshal, is a man tormented but faithful to his old allegiance.

The analogy between Arthur and John Lackland is curious. The attitude toward Arthur throughout the *Mort Artu* is reverent, and is based on the assumption that Arthur is a noble being. Yet here is a man whose act of incest pursues him, inspiring him with such hatred for his ill-begotten son that he is blinded to his own interests. Capable of burning a wife taken in adultery but eventually willing to receive her back, he first finds that his honor requires him to take vengeance on Lancelot in spite of prudent counsel to the contrary, but later he becomes most reluctant to pursue the culprit. No chronicler of the time of King John speaks reverently of him or assumes nobility in his character; at best there are sometimes indications of respect for his office as king. The man whom the chroniclers depict is treacherous, as Arthur never is; but the shifts from one extreme to the other, the tendency to allow hatred to outweigh self-interest, the willingness at times to let bad counsellors prevail over good, these tendencies characterize both the Arthur of the *Mort Artu* and John Lackland. The monarchs, with treachery left out of consideration, are much alike; the fictional idealization is not so much a matter of heightening good qualities as of omitting the worst.

Gawain's part in the *Mort Artu* after his brothers are killed is, until he lies on his deathbed, that of a relentless avenger. Ideologically, his behavior brings out the disastrous effects of a persistence in a blood feud. Forgetting this thesis, we can see him simply as an individual bent on the ruin of a great man against whom he has no just reason for enmity. Gawain is still the most valiant knight after Lancelot, the son of King Lot and King Arthur's nephew, a prince held in high esteem. His behavior has certain resemblance to that of Meiler Fitz Henry, in 1207 and 1208 William Marshal's enemy in Ireland.

Meiler, like Gawain, was a blood relative of the king. He was the son of an illegitimate son of Henry I, consequently a first cousin of King John's father, Henry II. Henry I's paramour was on this occasion Nesta, the daughter of the Prince of South Wales. Meiler was among the earliest and most prominent in the conquest of Ireland. For many years King John bestowed favors upon this cousin, though eventually he abandoned him. Giraldus Cambrensis highly lauds Meiler's valor and physical might:

corpore . . . pervalido, pectore quadrato, ventreque substricto, brachiis ceterisque membris ossosis, plus nervositatis habentibus quam carnositatis. Miles animosus et aemulus; nihil unquam abhorrens, quod aggredi quis vel solus debeat vel comitatus; primus in praelium ire, ultimus conserto praelio redire consuetus. In omni conflictu omnis strenuitatis opera, seu praeire paratus seu perire, adeo impatiens et praeceps, ut vel vota statim, vel fata complere dignum ducat, inter mortis et martis triumphos nihil medium ponens; adeo laudis cupidus et gloriae, quod si vivendo forte non valeat vincere velit vel moriendo. Vir itaque laude dignus. (R21 V.324)

A man thus praised for his valor could well come to mind as an analogue to Gawain. Even though Meiler's procedures as the enemy of William Marshal were underhanded instead of being forthright as are Gawain's against Lancelot, a pronounced similarity lies in this: each persuaded his king into action against a noble and involuntary enemy. Gawain insists on an expedition against Lancelot in Gaunes and stubbornly requires the continuation of its pursuit. Meiler, who was grand justiciar of Ireland, in a small company of John's favorites, spoke thus to the king:

> Sire, unques ne vos esmaiez;
> De los guerre seür seiez.
> Laissiez mei aler en Irlande
> Ge[s] vos metrai en tel kemande,
> Que par mei, que par mes amis,
> Qu'a Londres les vos rendrai pris.
> Isi les vos cuit justisier. (GM 13601–7)

His scheme was to retain Marshal in England and to have all his enemy's most important lieutenants summoned to the royal court. During their absence from Ireland he would seize the earl's lands. The plan failed because William Marshal's friends refused to leave Ireland. They gathered allies and crushed Meiler, who then fell into disgrace and was replaced about the end of 1208 as justiciar. Then came Meiler,

> Qui out esté cruel et f[i]ers
> En plorant, a merci al conte,
> Quer de sa mespresure out honte. (GM 14124–27)

William, while requiring a castle as guarantee of good behavior, pardoned him. Marshal's generosity and Meiler's repentance have a similarity to Lancelot's magnanimity and Gawain's final avowal of his "outrage" (172.30).

Though Meiler's personality and behavior offer a rather consistent analogue to Gawain's in the final episodes of the *Mort Artu*, Meiler left the stage too soon to fill out all the rôle that belonged to Gawain. As a group, King John's favorites were hostile to William Marshal. John de Grey, bishop of Norwich and John's unsuccessful candidate against Stephen Langton for the archbishopric of Canterbury, was no exception. He succeeded Meiler as chief justiciar of Ireland and as such pursued Marshal for harboring William de Braose. In May, 1213, he and Marshal were companions at arms against the expected, but eventually diverted, invasion of Philip Augustus. After resigning the justiciarship that year, he left on a mission to Rome for John and died in 1214. He, like Gawain, was faithful to a threatened king to the end, and died in the midst of civil torment without participating in the most critical events. Though no single Justiciar of Ireland offers a complete parallel to Gawain's behavior, successive Grand Justiciars in Ireland complete the analogue to Gawain's late career. After the trait of treachery is abstracted from these historical figures, their similarity to Gawain, like the similarity of John to Arthur, is great.

If there is a likeness between the Arthur of the *Mort Artu* and John Lackland, and a likeness between Gawain and two of John's courtiers, we may expect similarity also between Guenevere and John's consort, Isabelle of Angoulême. In Chrétien's *Charrette* and the Prose *Lancelot*, Guenevere's love is sublimated. In the *Mort Artu*, her abandonment of "fin amour" for "fol amour," for blind, shameless, and imprudent pursuit of passion, seems strange despite the character given her in Marie de France's *Lanval*, hints of like nature in the works of Geoffrey and Wace, and the influence of the *Tristan* legend. Her conduct was probably more easily understandable to a public cognizant of the reports concerning Queen Isabelle. Like Arthur, John was supposed to have imprisoned his queen for flagrant adultery (see p. 111*n*). Both queens were eventually freed, though under entirely different circumstances; after their husbands' deaths both disappear from the history, factual and legendary, of Great Britain.

Guenevere, after renouncing love, displays qualities unlike Isabelle's. When Mordred attacks her in the Tower of London, her courage and skill in supporting a siege have no basis in literary tradition. Furthermore, historical examples of such female exploits are rare. Perhaps we have here another echo of Eleanor of Aquitaine's experience at Mirebeau,[1] but a still apter case occurred during the troubles that we have been examining at the end of the reign of King John. Nicolaa de Haye held out at Lincoln against the forces hostile to young Henry III. Guenevere's successful strategy is carefully prepared and competently executed like Nicolaa's at Lincoln. For the siege of Guenevere another example in history complements the one just cited. When William Marshal departed from Ireland in obedience to King John's summons in 1207, he left his wife and lands in charge of his liegemen, some of whom were bent on treason. As in the *Mort Artu* and in Geoffrey's and Wace's works, when Arthur has put his wife and kingdom in charge of traitorous Mordred, rebellion results. Like Guenevere, William's countess participated in the hostilities. Her forces were victorious so that afterward her movements, like Guenevere's, were free.

In most respects we should seek nowhere in the history of the thirteenth century for an analogue to Mordred, for his rôle in its essentials is in the *Brut* and the *Historia Regum Britanniae*. Certainly, Louis of France was no Mordred. His behavior in England may be likened rather to that of Mordred's foreign allies than to that of the revolting chieftain himself. Still the march of his forces westward from London was like Mordred's. In the pseudo-Map Cycle, Mordred becomes Arthur's son. Sons rising against their father recur repeatedly in history, but the nearly contemporary example of the sons of Henry II must have rendered Mordred's rebellion more impressive. The fragments of analogy already adduced suggest that Mordred's whole rôle, as tailored to make it credible to the readers of the *Mort Artu,* is a composite in much the same way as Claudas's in the *Benoic-Gaunes*. Here are other elements that may have been woven into the fabric. John's illegitimate daughter, Joan, was the wife of Prince LLewellyn. The Welsh son-in-law was in a constant state of struggle against all Normans, John included. In 1212 while the king was campaigning against him, Joan sent word to her father that treachery was breeding.

---

[1] Perhaps the following passage of the *Mort Artu* on Guenevere was inspired by Eleanor of Aquitaine: "Meismes qu'ele iert bien en l'aage de cinquante anz estoit ele si bele dame que en tout le monde ne trouvast l'en mie sa pareille" (4.20–23). The bizarre emphasis on Guenevere's age is most easily explained as an early detail of the Cyclic Plan inserted at the instance of courtiers who wished to persuade Eleanor that beauty could exist in aged women, just as, they were maintaining, such was true with her.

Arthur receives a similar message from Guenevere. The leading traitor in 1212 was Robert Fitz-Walter, who later in 1216 was the commander of the rebel forces against King John. In legend and with some historians Fitz-Walter acquired good repute by being prominent among those who won the Magna Charta, but many considered him criminal. No one doubts that he was plotting treason in 1212, also earlier in 1204 when John lost Normandy. For his contemporaries this devious rebel, as distinguished from the open champions of revolt, must have made the Mordred of the *Mort Artu* more credible.

Lancelot's kindred, the "lineage Ban," are frequent actors in the *Mort Artu*, particularly Bohort. They are his principal advisers, his lieutenants, and his favorite companions, more cautious and less magnanimous than their chief. Their faithfulness recalls that of William Marshal's household, particularly when its members supported him in Ireland during the troubles of 1207–1212. The reminiscences of their fidelity to be found in the *Mort Artu* seem greatest in the battle before Joyous Guard (more or less parallel to the campaign against Meiler's adherents) and in the siege that follows (in some sort recalling the conduct of William's friends during the crisis when Marshal harbored William de Braose). The probability of reminiscence approaches certainty when in the romance the besieged deliberate the surrender of Guenevere. Lancelot agrees to giving her up in a manner that Bohort calls "moult legiere" (118.43), though his cousin's consent has come with tears and protestations of enduring love. Lancelot is acting solely at the dictates of honor—Guenevere's. Bohort predicts regret, and the others are in accord that the action would be bad, ending their protest thus: " 'Sire, quel poor avez vos del roi que vos madame li rendés?' " (118.57–58). When King John asked Marshal for his second son as a hostage, the earl called in his wife and "sa plus privee gent."

> A cel conseil li deloérent
> E distrent [que c'ert] felonie
> E qu'il ne l'i enveiast mie. (GM 13392–94)

William, like Lancelot, decided against advice and his own desires. His followers, in counseling him, further endangered themselves to advance the cause of their chief in the same way as the Clan of Ban. The result was the same.

Lancelot, Bohort, Lionel, Hector, and their forces defeat Mordred's sons before Winchester. After the main action the forces from Benoic and Gaunes are separated from Lancelot, who has pursued the "conte de Gorre" (198.29–30). In 1217 Louis's men, still in possession of Winchester, were attacked by William Marshal, his son William, and William Longsword, who was the younger Marshal's closest friend: "Il s'entramoient com[e] frére" (GM 15884). Though Richard Marshal was still too young for chroniclers to note his presence, quite conceivably he was with his father and brother. After a great measure of success the younger leaders, leaving the completion of victory to their elder, departed. Both in the *Mort Artu* and in 1217 a loyalist army, after the death of a king of Britain, defeated a rebel force at Winchester. The loyalist leaders were a family group; their chief separated from the others when victory was assured. The Clan of Ban and the Marshal group were all dead within a few years after the exploit at Winchester. The great earl died in 1219, his cousin of Salisbury in 1226, his sons in 1231 and 1234—Richard, like Lionel, from a wound received in a pitched battle.

In studying the *Benoic-Gaunes* our attention was drawn to the younger Marshals as parallels to youthful Bohort and Lionel when they were prisoners of Claudas. It should be no surprise, therefore, to find the two pairs of brothers again acting in parallel rôles. Throughout the *Mort Artu* Lancelot's cousins are so welded to him that the blood tie seems as close as that of William Marshal to his sons. Hector, half-brother to Lancelot, and the remaining member of the Clan of Ban, was more closely akin to Lancelot than Longsword to the great Marshal; the two earls were cousins only by marriage. To be exact, the father of Ela, countess of Salisbury, was Marshal's first cousin. She was the granddaughter of that Patrick whose death in Poitou we considered while dealing with the uncle-nephew relationship of Pharien and Lambegue (p. 45). An obvious reason for coupling Hector and the earl of Salisbury is that they were both the illegitimate sons of kings. The "lineage Ban" included a bastard, like the tight alliance of close friends and kindred about the great Earl Marshal.[2]

---

[2] Though irregular origin in a fabled hero is a rather common characteristic, leniency toward illegitimacy of birth in the pseudo-Map Cycle (when not the result of incest) is so marked that it might lead to a suspicion that the influence of William Longsword was great, for thirteenth-century bastards did suffer penalties. To be sure, Longsword became an earl, but his son did not inherit the title with his lands. Another of Henry II's extramarital achievements, Geoffrey, though ultimately archbishop of York, had difficulty in becoming a bishop. The benevolence of the Cycle toward bastards is manifest in other instances than that of Galahad. In the *Queste*, Hector is accorded much

The parts of the pseudo-Map Cycle that contain a well-defined geography based upon reality sometimes, as in the case of the *Mort Artu,* provide well-informed readers with points of reference from which they can spring into the unknown. Those readers of the *Benoic-Gaunes* capable of recognizing the disguised setting would have been fewer, though the Fontevrists and the noble ladies who, like Eleanor of Aquitaine, retired to live with them would have been able to explain the background to their widely disseminated relatives and thus have made the work a subject of conversation.

A basis in real geography allowed the writers to compose with a surer touch; at least the parts of the Cycle where the geography is based upon actuality are among those that the ages have acknowledged as effective. While complete abandonment of topographic probabilities, as in the *Queste,* may also aid in achieving successful literary effects, interest in passages recounting movements in space may slacken when there is no sense of either geographic reality or unreality.

Similar remarks may be made in regard to historical reminiscences, but in their case the effectiveness of reader recognition becomes of much greater importance. The verisimilitude of papal interference in royal marital affairs would be apparent to readers in all Europe, and would doubtless call up associations that would quicken interest. In like manner, the similarity between the situation of young Bohort and Lionel threatened by the power of Claudas and that of the youth Arthur Plantagenet in the hands of King John would be lost upon few in any public which the romances could reach; the emotions aroused would add to the power of the narrative. The perception of likenesses between fictional events and the happenings in the career of William Marshal might titillate only a small number of readers, but it is possible that such readers might be those most important to the author.

As time went on and recognition of similarities between news items of distant occurrence and the fictional episodes of the pseudo-

---

better treatment than the other "reprovés," among whom were Lionel and Gawain. He is allowed to come to the very door of the Grail Castle. The invention of a half-brother for Lancelot, fruit of King Ban's adultery, seems to have been a part of the revision of the Cyclic Plan at the beginning of the main period of composition. The *Mort Ban* with its pathos partly based on family would be less impressive if we suspected that the broken king had been guilty of infidelities toward his sainted wife. Explain Galahad's bastardy as you will, it is still true that the authors could have contrived a marriage ceremony for Lancelot and Pelles's daughter as easily as cohabitation without it; so also for the union of Bohort and Brangiore's daughter, who bears a future emperor of Constantinople.

Map Cycle diminished or vanished, the parts of the romances containing them in most cases maintained their attraction to readers. King Ban, who died of grief as he looked back on towers and steeples tumbling in flames, no longer recalled to readers the bitterness of Henry II, who, mortally stricken with disease, turned in his flight to gaze back on burning Le Mans; but Ban still remains a tragic figure. The author was still communicating the emotions that the inspiration of fact had stirred within him. But something was lost, the sense that naked history was there to fortify what imagination had created. For me the lost has now been found.

The geography of the *Benoic-Gaunes* must soon have passed from anyone's perception. All that ordinarily remains in its readers is a certain confidence in the author's sureness in depicting movements, a skill that he attained through his familiarity with the terrain of which he was writing. The effects of masterful use of a broader and better-known topography may remain. Those who can envisage Arthur's last campaign in spatial terms must, in the rush of two armies across southern England to meet a deathly appointment with Fortune, experience a sharper pang than those to whom marches from Dover to Salisbury Plain and from London to Salisbury Plain mean nothing.

The *Benoic-Gaunes*, which recounts the boyhood of Lancelot, and the *Mort Artu*, which treats of his last years, are the two sections of the pseudo-Map Cycle furnished with a geography referrable to reality and replete with reminiscences of events in history. The geography in question is that of the dearest possessions of the Angevin monarchs— that is, the border of Anjou and Poitou and southern England. The history is that of the late years of Henry II and of the reigns of his two sons, extending only slightly beyond.

The man who wrote the *Claudas-Frolle* is interested in the same period, with an interest Capetian and not Plantagenet. The author of the *False Guenevere* seems familiar with Flemish affairs. There are in these sympathies and familiarities at once a concentration and a dispersion that invites me to propose a solution to the puzzle.

6 ❦ A Hypothesis on the Manner of Fabrication of the Pseudo-Map Cycle

hile the foregoing chapters have treated the relations between the pseudo-Map Cycle and the world with which its earliest readers were acquainted, this chapter is concerned with problems in the fabrication of the Cycle. It hypothesizes about the manner of composition of the Cycle, examining first inferences that may be drawn from the Cycle alone in view of the literary fashions of the time, and afterwards supporting the hypothesis with the historical and geographical details discussed earlier or others of similar nature.

According to the generally received opinion, despite F. Lot, several authors wrote the pseudo-Map Cycle. Jean Frappier's contention that there was an *architecte* is reasonable, though I shall suggest modifications. I prefer to think of a powerful and resourceful chairman guiding an ideologically diversified group in the making of a complex plan.

Before investigating further these postulates for our Cycle, it is well to cast an eye over the twelfth- and thirteenth-century literary (not political, economic, and so forth) scene to discover whether there are other examples of literary or related activities in which contrasting views were united to provide a single work. The *Roman de la Rose* is such a work; chronological considerations remove any suspicions that Guillaume de Lorris and Jean de Meung planned it together. For the present purpose, what is important in this example is the proof that the public had a taste for extensive works with such contrasts written by more than one individual.

The element of length is necessarily absent from lyric poetry, but the taste for units containing contrasting notions is well exemplified by the *jeu parti*. This genre implies the existence of a social group interested at once in the subject debated and in the application of a literary (in this case poetic) technique to its treatment. The group was unified by its interest in the technique and in play with ideas, but like the authors it was presumably in amiable disagreement as to the acceptability of the ideas.

The introduction to Chrétien's *Charrette* makes it quite clear that a person who was not the author controlled the content, both ideological and narrative. We are justified in saying that the *Charrette* is Chrétien's, but at the same time we should remember that the poem is the result of a collaboration, even as regards redaction, since Godefroi de Leigni completed it, quite evidently according to a plan already worked out with Marie de Champagne and her court. Other great feudal personages may well have intervened to a similar extent in the fabrication of other works.

The taste for literary exposition of contrasting ideas in a single work written by more than one person existed at the period of the composition of the pseudo-Map Cycle, and a patron's control over an Arthurian work with at least dual authorship is a matter of record. The reader has doubtless already concluded that I am about to maintain the probability that the pseudo-Map Cycle was written by a group of authors with divergent views forced into cooperation by a great patron who contributed something for both *sens* and *matière*. Yes, but with complications as regards both patronage and direction.

Granted that the pseudo-Map Cycle is a debate presented under the form of narratives, the question at issue may be stated thus: Resolved, that courtly love is socially ideal and spiritually valuable, negligible in sinfulness and not harmful to society. The affirmative team debating this question would be required to show that not only the lovers, but also society, was bettered by courtly love. The negative team's task would be to demonstrate that it brought ruin to the lovers' souls, to those dear to the lovers, and to society as a whole. In order to gain as many interested readers as possible, this work of social philosophy should be an Arthurian romance, with roots among celebrated authors in that field. The general agreement would be that the Arthurian themes already existent in the works of Geoffrey of Monmouth and Wace and in the poems of Chrétien de Troyes should be developed as a means of presenting the argument. The affirmative would utilize primarily Chrétien's *Charrette*; the negative, his Grail theme created in *Perceval* and also the matter originating in the *Historia Regum Britanniae* and Wace's *Brut*. For the negative, a division of labor based on the two principal sources was evident. A further division of the Grail theme into a section demonstrating the sacredness of the Holy Vessel through its early history and a section expounding its victory over courtly love was easy to conceive. Generally accepted traditional morality should win; else representatives of the negative would withdraw from the game. Therefore, their case must have the last word. Fortunately, the Wace-Geoffrey source, by doing away with King Arthur, required the same approach.

The early history of the Grail, concerned to demonstrate in detail its Christian character, would go back to the Crucifixion and come first in the work. To balance this, the affirmative would have an early history, first of Arthur, then of Lancelot. By way of further balance in the distribution, the advantageous presentation of courtly love should relate as one of its elements the history of the establishment of the love, and as another a record of its enduring ennoblement. Finally, there should be a transitional section before the Arthurian Grail story in which the affirmative should still speak while the negative themes were introduced.

The clarity or the need for these divisions would not have appeared to all members of the teams of authors participating, and, I hypothesize, there would have been false starts. The works thus created, after rejection by the team of authors, would later appear as separate works earlier in date of composition than the accepted cycle, displaced but still closely allied to the original plan. Such works would be the *Perlesvaus* and Robert de Boron's *Joseph* (see Appendix).

After these observations based upon the ideological aspects of the Cycle with no consideration for what historical reminiscences and geographical allusions reveal, investigation of the probabilities as to how, where, when, and by whom the work was accomplished becomes more profitable.

Granting that there were several authors of the pseudo-Map Cycle, it seems almost necessary that there should have been a developed plan, written out and probably subject to expansions and revisions.[1] The

---

[1] To those who say that my hypothesis merely resurrects the theories of Jessie Laidlay Weston and Ernst Brugger concerning lost cycles, I will reply that, while acknowledging kinship between their speculations and mine, I attribute much more probability to mine. Leaving aside my support from historical and geographical allusions appearing

existence of such a preliminary outline may be supported by much of F. Lot's *Etude*; what Lot says to convince us of the truth of his belief in the existence of a single author may not advance his cause, but it does show that planning was done in such detail that without a written guide several authors would have been unable to follow it (pages 17 to 85 of the *Etude* are those most important in this connection).

If the Cycle existed in more-or-less developed outline before becoming a narrative for readers, we should expect to find in its less-polished portions bits that would be practically copies of the outline. Jean Frappier cites this passage:

> La damoisele . . . pensa toutes voies a la grant biaute lancelot . Et en celui pense li descendoit au cuer vne si grant amor . que elle ama lancelot outre chou que femme nama onkes si homme . Si li est auis que sil lamoit que elle seroit bone euree . Mais chi endroit nen parole plus li contes . mais cha auant vous deuisera comment elle lama merueilleusement . Et comment elle li pria . et la meruelle que sez amis en fist . quant il sot que elle lama . Et comment elle morut por chou quil le refusa" (IV.282.37–283:2).

Frappier says first that the maid of Escalot theme "a pu être suggéré" by these lines, and then "il serait bien impertinent de voir dans ce sec et plat *avertissement* une source de la fine et tragique histoire de

---

in the Cycle as it now exists, here in my favor is one additional argument (and there are others): It is more likely that notes not intended for preservation should be destroyed than that every page of a completed Cycle should disappear.

J. D. Bruce's theory of interpolations is also akin to my hypothesis. He assumes, however, that the interpolations were inserted into a completed work, whereas I hold that his "interpolations" are either the planned contributions accepted by an author from others working on the project or matter introduced by the author in obedience to the specifications of a prepared outline. If they are interpolations in the full sense of the word, it is strange that no strain of manuscript traditions exists without them.

Gweneth Hutchings in her edition of the Prose *Lancelot*'s *Conte de la Charrette* (Paris, 1838) builds up no theory concerning the composition of the whole cycle, but she vigorously rejects the notion that the *Charrette* section is an "addition interpolée . . . . Préparé de loin [le conte] occupe dans l'histoire sa place prescrite" (p. liv). By the apparent contradiction between an assertion on p. xlix–l that the tale is rewritten to show the sinfulness of *amour courtois* and a statement on p. lvii that the author "n'est pas préoccupé par l'idée de l'amour coupable de Lancelot et Guenièvere," she means to say that the writer who executed the *remaniement* was following a plan prepared for him which did not express his own convictions, that his source was both Chrétien's romance and an ideological outline imposed upon him. As I would state it, a member of the affirmative team working on the Cycle was mechanically carrying out specifications that the negative had succeeded in inserting into the Cyclic Plan.

A Hypothesis on the Manner of Fabrication of the Pseudo-Map Cycle

la demoiselle d'Escalot" (FEt 209). I hope that he would not object to seeing in it a misplaced note among the plans for the Cycle. Similar bits in other *avertissements* may be cited; the confusion of the passage on the Grail hero (III.29) is a case in point.

Prophecies may contain revealing bits. Mordred murders the "homme uestu de robe de religion" (V.283.42) who predicts that the son will kill the father. Lancelot takes from the dead man's hand a letter containing a prophecy addressed to Mordred and fulfilled in the *Mort Artu*: Arthur "te ferra parmi le cors si durement que apres le cop passera li rais du soleil" (V.285.27–28). The prophecy concludes, "apres cel iour ne sera nus qui le roy artu uoie se ce nest en songe" (V.285.30–31). The separation of the prophecy into a spoken and a written part suggests that the author had at hand a written version to which he was obliged to refer when he had exhausted his memory. The written version could not have been the completed *Mort Artu* because Arthur does not die on the day that he is wounded; he is alive all through the next morning and into the afternoon. His last day contains such notable events that if the author of the passage on Mordred had read them in the account that we have, he could not have forgotten them. Thus, he must have had only notes to guide him rather than the developed version. Conversely, if the author of the *Mort Artu* had known how the prophecy was expressed in the *Agravain*, he would have demanded a change.

References to episodes occurring earlier sometimes exhibit an awareness of the main course of events without displaying knowledge of the details set down anteriorly. Such a phenomenon may be explained as knowledge of an outline without knowledge of a completed account (either because there was not yet a full version or because its composition was taking place elsewhere). This state of affairs is particularly likely if not many pages separate the main recital from the next allusion. In such a case bad memory can hardly be alleged as an explanation. An example consists of the treatment of Banin. The *Mort Ban* recounts the stubborn resistance of Banin besieged in the keep at Trebes and his later vengeance upon Ban's treacherous seneschal. Near the end of the *Benoic-Gaunes* he is victor in a tournament and reminds Arthur of the fate of Ban. He is introduced as "vns cheualiers dont li contes parole cha en ariere" (III.108.35). But he has characteristics of which we have earlier learned nothing. He is here labeled a godson of Ban and is qualified with this epithet whenever he reappears in the Cycle. He "estoit vns petis cheualiers . si estoit a merueilles apers &

vistes . & de merueilleuse forche . Il auoit guerroie le roi claudas moult longuement & maint grant damage li auoit fait . Et tant auoit prins del sien & tant gaaignie al gueroier que richement & a bel harnois sen estoit partis de la terre" (III.108.37–41). There is neither here nor later any hint of events at Trebes or on the field below Benoic, no reference to Claudas's efforts to retain him. The *Mort Ban* must already have been written, but the author of the rest of the *Benoic-Gaunes* apparently had at his disposition only an outline.

References to events occurring earlier may also contain features not included in the original recital. In the *Mort Artu* the Roman emperor attacking Arthur declares: "Sui ça venuz por vengier un nostre prince, Frolle d'Alemaigne" (160.58–59). In the *Claudas-Frolle* where the Romans play a large part, no mention is made of Roman connection with Frolle. His presence is explained by the anarchy in Gaul because the barons could not agree on a successor to their dead king: "Pour le grant descort quil auoient longement maintenu . . . fu uenus vns quens dalemainge e[n]treuls que len appeloit frolle . et auoit grant plente auec lui dalemans . quar il auoit beance dauoir le royaume" (V.370.37–40). The connection with the Romans, originating in Geoffrey, must have been specified in the outline as a motivation for the Romans' war on Arthur, and was simply neglected by the author of the *Claudas-Frolle*, who was indifferent to the need that the *Mort Artu* had for it (see 160.59).

There are indications that necessary details of the *Mort Artu* were understood at the time of the composition of the *Benoic-Gaunes*, which can only have been true through the existence of an outline. In the *Mort Artu* it is necessary that Lancelot have a Continental kingdom to which he may withdraw; his patrimony must have been regained. The reconquest takes place in the *Claudas-Frolle* section of the *Agravain*, but it is foreshadowed in the *Benoic-Gaunes*. The Black Monk who reassures the bereaved queens as to the fate of their sons goes to Arthur's court and upbraids him for abandoning his liegeman Ban. Arthur acknowledges his obligation and promises to "si bien amender que nus ne men pora blasmer sa son tort non" (III.47.28–29).

All authors could not be expected to find the prepared outline of the Cycle to their taste. For the *Claudas-Frolle*, I guess at such a situation because of the treatment of women and the unheroic share given Lancelot. The outline probably required that Lancelot, justly furious at Claudas's behavior toward Guenevere and her messengers, should gather forces and recover his patrimony with the aid of the Lady of the

Lake, and that, at a new threat to him, Arthur encouraged by Guenevere should bring reinforcements. Such a plan is consistent with the
spirit of the Cycle; Lancelot, Guenevere, and the Lady of the Lake
would all behave admirably and importantly. The episode as written,
though violating the Cyclic spirit, accomplishes all the narrative aims
of this supposed plan. The demotion of Lancelot from a hero into a
parasite was presumably undertaken by a man who ought to have
been on the negative team in the debate, who regarded courtly love as
nearly despicable and denied its stimulation to noble deeds. He also
tended to regard women as at best ornamental. Guenevere serves the
plot as she should but can influence no one but her lover. For the last
appearance of the Lady of the Lake in the Cycle, it seems likely that the
makers of the outline intended an impressive act. Instead she performs
a part that might have been assigned to any squire or wandering
damsel. As she travels back home from a state visit to the camp of
Gawain, Bohort, and Lionel, she happens to see Romans in a wood
and returns with the news, then departs. In some manuscripts she is
allowed no later appearance; in others, after Lancelot's arrival two
lines are given to a second visit for her, a complete anticlimax. The
original intention must have been that Lancelot should campaign from
the beginning, with the lady bringing him potent aid. The treatment
of Lancelot's mother also seems a trifle degrading; she visits her son at
Gaunes (her death soon afterward is noted). For Lancelot to visit her
and his father's tomb would have been more dutiful. The *Claudas-
Frolle* must have been part of the original design for the pseudo-Map
Cycle, but the episode could hardly have been executed by a writer
who had the same ideals as those which the team for the affirmative
had had in mapping out these events. The testimony points to an outline extending the length of the Cycle and developed later in detail—at
some times more faithfully than at others.

The *Mort Ban* seems to have been written for someone greatly
impressed by the death of Henry II. The historical background of the
Mort Artu seems concentrated on the final years of the reign of King
John. Even though the circumstances of Henry's death were so impressive that they could be long remembered (in contrast to the confusion of events in the period surrounding 1216, a confusion such that
reminiscences from it would have endured a much shorter time), still,
the writing of the Cycle, excluding the *Merlin* Continuations, must
have gone on over a rather long period of time—fifteen, twenty, twenty-
five years. Consequently, with the political shifts in the first third of

the thirteenth century, the original patron was very likely replaced by successors.

There seems a strong feminine influence in the pseudo-Map Cycle, not merely of the kind that finds its greatest interest in the conquest of a man's love, but of such a sort as to make of women independent agents influencing behavior outside amorous domains. One can perceive it at work in the *Mort Artu*, particularly when Guenevere defends herself against Mordred; it is present, though veiled, in the *Claudas-Frolle,* and is salient in the *False Guenevere*, which is essentially a political struggle between two women who gather partisans about them. It is most evident in the *Benoic-Gaunes.* Though the two queens, widows of King Ban and King Bohort, are essentially passive figures, one is the founder of an abbey. The Lady of the Lake, her damsels, and Pharien's wife are of a different type. The characteristics of the first and the last, as we have seen, appear to contain reminiscences of traits exhibited by Eleanor of Aquitaine; that is, they are women of action who help to form events. The same may be said of Saraide, who spirits away the princes after mingling as an actor in a tumultuous episode, and of her replacement who goes from the lake abode to learn the fate of Pharien and Lambegue. The latter damsel is one of the negotiators who arranges the investigating mission of Lambegue and Leonce, and something more than a guide as she leads them toward the lake: she tells them what they may and may not do.

If we compare these rôles of the *Benoic-Gaunes* with those of women not motivated by love in preceding Arthurian literature, we find little that is similar. The women of Marie de France are given major parts to play, but nearly always strictly in matters of love. The Guenevere of *Lanval* is to some degree an exception, but her plotting against the hero is the result of a baffled amour. In the *Tristan* love is the whole matter. In the works of Chrétien de Troyes it is still love in or out of marriage that leads to whatever feminine political participation there is. In the rest of the Vulgate Cycle, particularly in the *Queste,* outside of the realms of love women are usually pawns—except for interventions of the Lady of the Lake, particularly through the muffled damsel in the conquest of Dolorous Guard (see *PMLA,* LXXXV [1970], 433–43). In the *Perlesvaus* the recurring bits assigned to the Damsel of the Cart make her mingle in extra-amorous affairs in ways that transcend passivity, but she does not exercise her will; she simply tells what must be.

After much consideration of these phenomena, I suggest Eleanor of Aquitaine as the original patron of the pseudo-Map Cycle. I do so only after hesitation, for there is a tendency to attribute literary influence to the queen even when substantiating evidence is small. Rita Lejeune assembles the testimony of influence and presents it as affecting works as follows:

1. those in which Eleanor's reputation seems to have influenced the content (*Pèlerinage de Charlemagne*, Lj 15);

2. those in which her tastes seem exemplified and arouse suspicions that the author wished to attract her attention (*Eneas*, Lj 21);

3. those in which no other patron is indicated and in which she is praised, but remains anonymous (poems of troubadours, Lj 17–20; *Roman de Troie*, Lj 22–24);

4. those in which another, particularly Henry II (or the young king), is indicated as patron, but for which Eleanor seems to have been the effective patron (*Lais* de Marie de France, Lj 38–40);

5. those in which she is called by her name or equivalent with implications that she is a patroness, but others too are named with the same implications (*Chronique ascendante* of Wace, Lj 26);

6. one work, Wace's *Brut* (Lj 25–26), for which there is testimony from another writer, Layamon,[2] that she was the patroness, though the poem itself indicates another.

Except in the last two cases Eleanor is not named outright. We are elsewhere obliged to depend upon circumstantial evidence, which, as in the case of the poems of Chrétien (Lj 29–30), may be quite fragile; the best attested case deals with Arthurian literature. I do not mean to reject the first four categories; they are of various degrees of probability. The case favoring Eleanor as a patron of troubadours is very strong. One may be attracted by the theory that the *Pèlerinage de Charlemagne* caricatures relations between Eleanor and Louis VII. The author must

---

[2] Layamon's affirmation that Eleanor sponsored Wace's *Brut* arouses a suspicion that he himself had received encouragement from the queen. It is probable that he was stimulated to make his remark by recent experience with her; it is even probable, since he makes an allegation concerning patronage that Wace himself does not make, that the Englishman received his information from the queen or her household rather than from the poet. Her years of imprisonment afforded her an opportunity, which a person of her temperament would hardly have neglected, for learning not only the English language but also something of Anglo-Saxon culture, so that she may have manifested benevolence in practical ways, especially while she was powerful from 1189 to 1194. Protection of Layamon, however slight it might have been, would show that her interest in Arthurian literature continued till late in life and would make her patronage of the pseudo-Map Cycle still more reasonable.

have thought that Eleanor's assertive tongue as novelized would attract listeners; similarly, the author of the *Benoic-Gaunes* must have
believed that an idealized Eleanor would bring in readers.

More important to the present purpose is a consideration of Eleanor's patronage of Wace's *Brut*. Layamon's assertion leaves no doubt
that she was a patroness of Arthurian pseudochronicle, and her
continued protection of Wace as demonstrated when he says in the
Chronique ascendante,

> Ne me funt mie rendre a la curt le musage;
> De duns et de promesses chascun[s] d'els m'assuage (vv. 20–21,
> Lj 26),

assures us that her interest was enduring.

There is no positive evidence that Marie de France was hiding
patronage by Eleanor behind mention of a king, though the example
of the *Brut* might lead one to think so, but at the very least Eleanor and
her ladies, as members of the royal court, must have been part of the
audience for them. The allusions of Andreas Capellanus are sufficient
proof that Eleanor was concerned in France with matters that gave
rise to tales and verse exemplifying courtly love. Marie's *Lais* combine
such a predilection with another one for events in Angevin domains.
Taking the taste for Arthurian pseudochronicle, *roman d'aventures*,
and Plantagenet geography together, we should not be surprised to
find Eleanor of Aquitaine initiating a scheme for a grandiose narrative
combining all three with ideological concerns of a sort to attract her.

In examining the connection of the *Benoic-Gaunes* with the Abbey
of Fontevrault, we saw that Eleanor retired to that abbey for most of
her last years, after having been its protectress since the year of her
marriage to Henry II. She must have had great interest in the abbey—
and its region. Where one kingdom for Ban and his family would
have served the purposes of the romance, as in the *Lanzelet*, the creation of two adjacent friendly kingdoms, Benoic and Gaunes, with close
family connections, confronting together an encroaching hostile power,
would naturally be the idea of a person in Eleanor's position, mistress
by birth of many provinces and joined by marriage and motherhood to
men ruling over other and vaster domains. The portrait of the Lady of
the Lake with its idealization suggests that there Eleanor is portrayed as
she herself probably directed. Perhaps the make-up of the household at
the magic lake could fit that of a few great ladies about 1200, but this

sentence by H. G. Richardson about Eleanor's retinue seems particularly adapted to what the romance depicts at the castle of the Lady of the Lake: "We could name her steward, her constable, her butler, her knights and sergeants, her almoners, her chaplains and clerks, some of her damsels, her nurse, her cooks, her ewerer" (Ri 208). Eleanor's biographers frequently speak of her as exercising specifically invested authority, but Richardson makes it clear that her power had no well-defined limits. She accomplished many things by the force of her personality and the prestige accorded her as the wife and mother of kings, just as the Lady of the Lake without constituted power affects events in the kingdom of Gaunes and at moments in Great Britain after Lancelot has gone there. Elspeth Kennedy has brought into relief how much the passage on the chivalrous ideal insists upon "personal effort and exercise of the will" (Ken 103). And feminism as well may be read into this line from the *Benoic-Gaunes*: "dun homme & dune feme sont issus toutes gens . Ie ne sai pas par quel raison li vn ont plus de gentilleche que li autre . se on ne la conquert par proeche" (III.89. 28–30). Such a woman as Eleanor had the resources and the influence to assemble the forces for an undertaking like the cycle. To imagine any other patron so interested in Fontevrault and at the same time capable of marshaling authors with opposing philosophies to write as a unit is difficult for me.

I conceive of her most important contribution as being the general plan. It seems an epitome of her life's interests. Every one accepts the opinion that she was interested in courtly love. How nearly her practice conformed to her theories it is hard to say. Whether or not the *médisants* were right, their tales make it certain that at the very least she had a history of conspicuous flirtations. Her political manipulations and her warlike exploits gave her background for imagining intrigues in courts and cities and adventures in the field. She remained active and keen to the end of her life; her participation in the campaign of 1202 at the age of eighty is proof of it. When she retired to Fontevrault in her seventies she had reached a time of life when religious considerations, promoted by the hope of a happy eternity, had become important to her, and when she could see objectively the follies caused by unbridled love, perhaps as exemplified in 1202 by her son John with the wife whom he had torn from her intended mate. The Prose *Lancelot* proper, then, expresses her past; the *Queste*, her concern for the future; and the *Mort Artu*, her disillusioned view of her present. I do not think that she had precisely in mind these works as they now exist, but her life might well lead her to conceive of three divisions showing an ideal extramarital love, an ideal repentance, and a social disaster bound up with *fol amour*.

Aside from her importance in determining the divisions of the Cycle and their general content, there is, I believe, a high probability that Queen Eleanor, besides being the patron, had much to do with determining the content of the *Benoic-Gaunes*. She could personally have directed the composition of something very like the present *Mort Ban*; indeed, I am very nearly convinced that she stood over the man who wrote not only of the death but also of the founding of the Moustier Royal so like unto Fontevrault. Beyond this point I would reduce her share to detailed planning. Thus she could have imagined shutting up King Bohort's relict in a castle like Mirebeau, just as she was herself caught in such a plight in 1202. She could have specified the character of Claudas and of the Lady of the Lake. She could have presided over a first redaction of the lady's treatise on chivalry (through page 40) and listened to a reading of this homily. She probably outlined all later incidents occurring at the lake abode. Inspired by her own intermittent relations with her own children from both beds, she could have imagined that the lady reared more than one disinherited prince, that Claudas should first have them, and then by the lady's intervention he should lose them. In the portrait of Claudas the traits like those of her favorite son, Richard, would probably not have received her approval; but that the *Benoic-Gaunes* should be pro-Plantagenet while the portrait depicted primarily an unflattered Henry could well have been by the suggestion of a woman who was hostile to Capetians but who had been imprisoned by King Henry. Indeed, the portrait has stylistic variations that suggest dual authorship or revision under different pressures from those cogent in an early version. Most of it is made of terse phrases. But the discourse on love inserted in it is in a much more flowing style with a number of subordinate clauses. It attempts delicate analysis; the rest of the portrait is deliberately rough-hewn. Delicacy and complication also mark somewhat the sentence describing Claudas below the neck. Now these two parts of the portrait are those that seem reminiscent of Richard; almost all the rest of the description recalls Henry II.

If the early planning of the pseudo-Map Cycle took place before the death of Eleanor, it is proper to delve into the question of whether Walter Map had some hand in it. The passage at the end of the *Queste* concerning the redaction of the romance says that "Mestre Gautier

Map" drew it from records in "l'almiere de Salebieres" (Q 280.1). The beginning of the *Mort Artu* says that at the command of King Henry "son seigneur" (1.4) "Mestres Gautiers Map" wrote "la mort le roi Artu" (1.10). Because Map died about 1210 it has been the custom (exemplified by Lot, LEt 126–29; and Bruce, BE I.368–73) to regard the attribution as Jean Frappier did in 1936, when he called it "fantaisiste" (FEt 20). In 1961, influenced by a paragraph (BM 29–30) in the introduction to André Boutemy's *Gautier Map, conteur anglais,* he is cautious: "Il se peut que la référence au conteur anglais ait une réalité qui nous échappe" (FEt 428). Boutemy suspects that Hugh of Rutland (Rotelande) about 1185 in his *Ipomedon,* by alluding to Walter Map's skill in lying, was referring, because of a context describing a three-day tournament, to Map's fictional creations in the Arthurian field. Others, analyzed by Bruce (BE I.371) with a refutation, had already commented on this possible interpretation of Hugh's joke. For my part I am inclined to believe that there is a spark of truth in the attribution, but only a spark. Map's genius, as expressed in *De Nugis Curialium,* the only work certainly his, produced scraps, not large masterful projects.

Walter Map probably saw little of Queen Eleanor during the reign of Henry II.[3] He seems early to have been attached to Becket rather than the king and is not known to have been in the royal service until

---

[3] The sole words concerning Eleanor in *De Nugis Curialium,* the only work certainly written by Walter, are defamatory; here they are: "[Concerning Henry] in quem iniecit oculos incestos Alienor Francorum regina, Lodouici piissimi conjux, et iniustum machinata diuorcium nupsit ei, cum tamen haberet in fama priuata quod Gaufrido patri suo lectum Lodouici participasset. Presumitur autem inde quod eorum soboles in excelsis suis intercepta deuenit ad nichilum" (Distinct V, Chap. 6, MNC 237.5–10 [Wright edition, p. 226]). One of the few references to contemporary events in *De Nugis Curialium* occurs at four pages' distance from the passage on Eleanor, its closeness indicating that it was then presumably composed at nearly the same time. It states that Boniface (Map should have said Conrad) of Montferrat was killed in Palestine in the presence of kings Richard and Philip (MNC 241.10–14). The murder took place in 1192 (Philip had already returned home). The inaccuracy of Map's report indicates how distant he was from news sources after the death of Henry II. It also gives the impression that when he wrote he knew very little about Eleanor and her authority in the period from 1189 to 1194; her power was distant. The impression is increased when Map says not a page beyond the description of Eleanor that Henry's troubles were all caused by his sons (MNC 237.13) and fails to name Eleanor.

We have no reason to believe that *De Nugis Curialium* became widely circulated. There is but one manuscript, and no allusions to the work in the medieval period have been reported. Eleanor may never have known that this particular man committed to writing the ancient slander against her. Even if she had read it, she is known to have overlooked other injuries and to have continued relations with the malefactor.

1173. Eleanor, then in revolt, was a prisoner in the following years. When she gained her liberty upon the death of her husband, Walter no longer had a position at court. But possibly Map and the queen were for a short time together after her retirement to Fontevrault.

In March, 1199, when Walter was a candidate for bishop in the diocese of Hereford, he and a delegation called upon St. Hugh, bishop of Lincoln, to persuade him to intercede in their favor with King Richard. The interview took place at Angers (R37 281). Queen Eleanor was then at Fontevrault, where she was to receive shortly afterward the news of Richard's death. Since Walter was soliciting Hugh's support in Angers, it is reasonable to suppose that he would have pleaded for Eleanor's at Fontevrault, only a few miles away. It is almost as reasonable to think that an ambitious candidate would do his best to convince a woman who might greatly help him that they had intellectual interests in common. Thus Walter and Eleanor would discuss the cyclic Arthurian project and perhaps sketch it. At any rate Walter Map's name would be left among the notes, where it might have escaped the attention of the writers of the Prose *Lancelot*.

The author of the *Mort Artu*, discovering the record, could not fasten the ascription to Map to those parts of the Cycle that others were composing, except by saying, "Si se test ore atant mestre Gautiers Map de l'*Estoire de Lancelot*" (204.8–9). The regular manuscript tradition alleges the authorship only in the passage cited. Since the sentence at the end of the *Queste* may have been appended, the attribution may be regarded as the work of the author of the *Mort Artu*. It was natural that he should do so, for the last section of the Cycle was written by a man who knew England, aiming at a public interested in England, and Walter Map was known, if at all, primarily in England; he was not an international celebrity. All medieval references to him except those excited by the ascription that we have been discussing are by Britons. Hugh of Rutland's name identifies him as a native of the same region as Walter. Giraldus Cambrensis was a fellow courtier in England. Other allusions to the author of *De Nugis Curialium* are by English chroniclers.

The statement in the *Mort Artu*, "si fu avis au roi Henri son seigneur que ce qu'il avoit fet ne devoit pas soufire" (1.3–5), ties the romance territorially to Plantagenet lands. Though chronology does not allow us to consider Henry II as the protector, the phrase affirms that the work had a patron; the affirmation should not be disregarded. It points to a connection with Eleanor of Aquitaine, the real patron of

Wace's *Brut*, a poem which, like the pseudo-Map Romances, announces its tie to King Henry.

To repeat, as I see it, Eleanor of Aquitaine was the initial patron and planner of the whole pseudo-Map Cycle, the close supervisor of a limited section at the beginning of the *Lancelot*, responsible also for many detailed features until the hero should become established as the best knight in the world.

The possibility that Isabelle of Angoulême, wife of John Lackland, was one of the later patrons of the Cyclic Project cannot be neglected. Except for her years as queen of England she lived her whole life in the general region of the *Benoic-Gaunes*. She too went into retirement at Fontevrault and is buried there. I incline to think that in her last years (she died in 1246) she was the direct patroness of the *Merlin* Continuations or of one of them; a part of these romances is set in the *Benoic-Gaunes* region with a geography, as we have seen (p. 4), similar to that of the beginning of the Prose *Lancelot*. While Isabelle was on the throne of England, she was without the maturity, and probably also the prestige, necessary to steer a complicated project, and for those years I do not regard her as a possible *animateur*. She may, however, well have dallied with the plans for it and helped keep it alive when imprisonment forced restricted physical activity upon her.[4]

Except for such desultory attentions in the period from the death of Eleanor in 1204 to the death of her son John in 1216, the Cyclic Project must very nearly have lain fallow without a powerful aristocratic patron and with troubled conditions general, especially about Fontevrault. Within the Cycle this period of quiescence is indicated by the nature of historical reminiscences. For instance, in the *Benoic-Gaunes* after the *Mort Ban* its author knew events that happened near the end of the reign of King John; it would be unreasonable to think that, without pause, he spent the years till then after Eleanor's death on

---

[4] Isabelle's imprisonment is a matter of debate. The more lurid accounts of her behavior originated late. Here are two cautious modern statements on the subject: "It is said that she also [as well as John] was guilty of infidelities and that the king put her lovers to death. In December, 1214, John ordered that she should be kept in confinement at Gloucester" (*Dictionary of National Biography*). "One chronicle [not specified] states that in 1208 she was placed in custody at Corfe and in December, 1213, Terric Teutonicus was ordered to take her to Gloucester and guard her in her chamber, in which she bore her daughter Joan, but neither of these necessarily implies imprisonment" (Sidney Painter, *Reign of King John* [Baltimore, 1949], p. 236). Painter may be right, but Corfe Castle served as a state prison for others (see note 5, below, for an example), and Gloucester would hardly be the choice of a queen for a lying-in.

one hundred pages. Interruption and resumption must be the explanation.

Whatever the channels of communication between the early period and the later, the sons of William Marshal—not the great earl himself, for he died in 1219—deserve consideration as probable later patrons of the Cyclic Project. The family sponsorship of the *Histoire de Guillaume le Maréchal* shows in his sons both an interest in literary patronage and veneration of their sire. The allusions to William's share in the events of 1189, and the general likeness between his problems and those sketched for Pharien by Eleanor and her friends, would have attracted them to the project. In both the *Benoic-Gaunes* and the *Mort Artu* the many reminiscences from William's later career, particularly its Irish phases, seem to show that the Marshals were occupied with the Cycle, for the information displayed suggests a source best explained as the Marshal family itself.

Though one son of the great earl rather than two may have protected the authors of the pseudo-Map Cycle, there is reason to think that both William, Jr., and Richard might have had a hand in it. I have suggested earlier that they furnished models for Lionel and Bohort. In the *Benoic-Gaunes* Lionel seems the older of the two; certainly he receives more attention from the author both at Gaunes and at the lake. He is more aggressive, endowed with much *fierté*. Though it is natural that a boy farther advanced in adolescence than his brother should be more apt to display such qualities, Lionel's marked *fierté* accompanies him through the Cycle, becomes the violence of a *reprové* in the *Queste*. Bohort, when the princes grow up, is the darling of the narrators, and in the *Mort Artu* is the spokesman of the Clan of Ban.

Since Lionel is the older, he should be the fictional form of William, and Bohort of Richard. A few facts concerning the Marshals can be alleged in support of the assumption. William had his moments of punctilio. In the short period when he served Louis of France, he objected so strongly to another's being named marshal of England in Louis's government that he gained his point, though he lost another urgent demand that he be given Marlborough Castle. His first wife died early; he then successfully clamored for the hand of Henry III's sister (after William's death the wife of Simon de Montfort). The *Histoire de Guillaume le Maréchal* says that when the great earl lay dying, he sent his son William to put the boy king into the hands of the papal legate. When William and his sovereign arrived at their destination, the bishop of Winchester was with the legate. This war-like and ambitious prelate

> Sailli sus, sil prist par la teste.
> Lors dist li gienvles Mar.
> Qui [fu] molt cortois et leials,
> "Sire evesque," dist il, "lassiez.
> Por niant vos i baessiez." (GM 18104-8)

To put it mildly, William was short-spoken. The trait appeared too when his second marriage was delayed. The bride-to-be was a child, the sister of Henry III. The earl demanded an immediate ceremony or freedom from his contract of marriage. Truly lamented by his young wife, the younger William died in 1231. Lionel is the first of the Clan of Ban to die. The shift in the Cycle of prominence from Lionel to Bohort might make one think that the *Benoic-Gaunes* was written before 1231 and that, beginning somewhere in Sommer's Volume IV, the rest of the Cycle was written afterward. Perhaps.

William, Jr., is named by the *Histoire de Guillaume le Maréchal* as the member of the Marshal family who gave the order for the work. Therefore, the author uses only the most laudatory language concerning him; he also praises all the other sons and daughters, from whom the poet evidently expected a handsome gift (GM 19201-9). In all this praise, however, it is possible to see some differentiation of characterization. In the passage of some length that the poem devotes to a description of the old earl's ten chidren, these are the verses on William:

> Li premier filz out non Will.
> Si vos di bien qu'en cest reame
> N'out nul, si com j'oï retraire
> Qui tant s'atornast a bien faire;
> Eisi l'oï a toz conter
> Bien deit a grant enor monter
> E enprendre une grant besoingne
> Cui l'om port tel testemoingne. (GM 14873-80)

The phrases "si com j'oï retraire" and "Eisi l'oï a toz conter" make the judgments expressed depend on public opinion and not on the writer's own. This caution suggests that perhaps William was not quite the same man in private.

The verses concerning Richard make no appeal to common report; on his own authority the poet speaks thus:

> E Ric., qui fu aprés nez,
> Out proesce e sens e bealtez
> E bones mors e gentillesce;
> Charité, enor e largesse
> Firent de lui tox dis lor oste;
> Molt valt qui de tel gent s'acoste. (GM 14883–88)

Among all the complimentary banalities here heaped together, I direct special attention to the words "sens" and "largesse"—the latter as evidence of the prospects that writers might have with Richard, the former as revealing intellectual interests.

The third brother, Gilbert, who was earl of Pembroke from 1234 to 1241, is accorded three verses in the passage on the family, which emphasize his "sens." He was evidently fitted to continue sponsorship of a cyclic literary project. Here are the verses:

> Gilibert fu li terz nomez;
> Clers fu, de boen senz renommez,
> De bones mors, de boen afaire. (GM 14889–91)

William and Richard were both accorded comments on character by Roger of Wendover in chronicling their deaths. Of William he says only: "In militia vir strenuus" (R84 III.10). Of Richard: "Miles egregius, in literali scientia sufficienter eruditus, moribus decenter et virtutibus ornatus" (R84 III). Contemporaries thus attribute to Richard qualities that fit him to be the model of Bohort and, more importantly, the patron of the writers producing the pseudo-Map Cycle.

The Marshals had lands on the Continent as well as in Great Britain and Ireland. King John's wrath in 1205 against the elder William was occasioned by the homage that Marshal had done to Philip Augustus for his French fiefs. His son Richard was particularly assigned to these and, at least from the time of his father's death in 1219 till that of his older brother in 1231, Richard spent most of his time on the Continent. His primary inherited holdings were at Orbec and Longueville in Normandy. By marriage he became lord of Dinan and viscount of Rohan, and he took part in Breton affairs. Thus he could well have become protector of writers for the Cycle who were unacquainted with England or with Anjou and Poitou and were Capetian in sympathies, as in the case of the author of the *Claudas-Frolle*. Despite his intimate association with affairs on both sides of the Channel, Richard seems to have thought of England and France as two independent entities. At least his quarrel with Henry III while he was earl of Pembroke was over the influence of "foreign" advisers upon the king. Such a man would have had no objection if one author spoke like a Frenchman, and another showed enthusiasm for England.

The Grail passage in Helinand's chronicle may contain a revelation of Marshal's protection of the Cycle on the Continent. The passage does not fully identify the "historia de gradali" to which it refers with one that we possess. The description is not appropriate to the *Perlesvaus* because it states that the "historia" concerned primarily Joseph of Arimathea's adventures with the Grail. It is not appropriate to the Cyclic *Estoire del Graal* because the revelation to the author was not made by Christ but by an "angelum." The claim of any revelation at all eliminates Robert de Boron's *Joseph*.

Yet the passage does speak of a "historia de gradali" revealed to a hermit, elusive to Helinand, even to his informants, but to be found among unidentified "proceribus." When Helinand says "tota" in the phrase "nec facile, ut aiunt, tota inveniri potest," we may infer that the "historia" was either in an unfinished state or circulated in parts. Chances are favorable that he is speaking of a rumor that had reached him concerning the Cyclic Plan and fragments developed from it, not wholly preserved later or not utilized without change.

Helinand says that the hermit lived "hoc tempore [ca. 720] in Britannia." No romance locates authorship in space as Helinand does. The latter may have chosen Britain as the place of the hermit's residence because he had heard that the "historia" was in part located there or, more likely, because the tale was said to have come from the island. The *Estoire* gives the year of revelation: "auint apres la passion nostre signor ihesu crist . vij . c . & . xvij" (I.4.1–2). Apparently, Helinand was apprised of something resembling this datum, but he differs from the *Estoire* by approximately the length of the life of Christ—more evidence that he was writing from information differing from that in the romances. In inserting the item at the point where he does, he was influenced, it seems, by the item just preceding, which says, with data precise, and not approximate, as in the Grail item: "[Vulfrannus] obiit apud Fontenellam xiii kal. Aprilis, anno domini 720. Sepultus est juxta beatum Wandregesilum in ecclesia Beati Pauli, in quo loco jacuit annis quadraginta, sanctus autem Ansbertus annis undecim" (Hel 814). This item and the appended Grail item are contained within the long entry for the year 718. The next entry is for 719, and, quoting from Bede, deals with events in Constantinople. The item on Saint Wandrille and the other saints bears the mark of propaganda from Fontenelle Abbey. The Grail is not included in the sales talk, but it must have come to Helinand from the same source; the insertion of the item at this point is not otherwise to be explained. It evidently reproduces gossip current at Fontenelle. People were talking of the "historia de gradali" in that part of Normandy where Richard Marshal held fiefs at the time that Helinand was writing late in the reign of Philip Augustus.

The Flemish or Picardian influence perceptible in the *False Guenevere* with its echoes of the False Baldwin episode points to authorship by someone in or from that region. The Cyclic *Estoire* and *Queste* seem to me to have been elaborated in the same general region, for I accept Bruce's contention that Corbenic is derived from Corbiniacum (Corbeny) and Mordrain from Maurdramnus (BE I.393–94; MLN 34 [1919].385 ff.). This northern influence can, like the Norman, be reconciled with the theory of patronage by the Marshal family. A very close friend of the great Earl Marshal was Baldwin of Béthune, third son of its *avoué*, who by marriage became Comte d'Aumale in Normandy with lands also in England. The friendship between the earl and Baldwin was so close that William Marshal Junior was betrothed to Baldwin's daughter with the provision that, should either of the betrothed die, the next younger son or daughter should take over the engagement. Baldwin's father also valued William Marshal highly. The Avoués de Béthune were "seigneurs protecteurs de Saint-Vaast d'Arras," a possible center for the diffusion of Grail literature; they also held lands in England (Ipm I.13, item 49). The wedding that sealed the alliance between the Béthune and Marshal families took place; but the bride died by 1224, at which time the widower remarried.

When Marie de France speaks of her *Fables* as written

> Pur amur le cunte Willalme
> Le plus vaillant de cest reialme [Epilogue, vv. 9–10],

she refers either to William Marshal the elder, earl of Pembroke, or to William Longsword, earl of Salisbury. Personally, because of dating probabilities, I favor Marshal over Longsword as Marie's patron, but whichever earl is meant, Marie's dedication provides evidence that she had found a patron in a man benevolent toward the Lancelot-Grail Cyclic project, for Longsword, even if not a direct sponsor, must be accounted sympathetic to it because of his close friendship with the William Marshals, father and son, and because of his figuration as Hector in the Clan of Ban. The earl of Salisbury's primary importance to the hypothesis that I have been advancing is that by the location of his earldom he offers a clear link between the Marshals and the Fontevrists, who had a house at Amesbury, so to speak, next door to Longsword's castle. Before studying Amesbury, I need to say more of the mother abbey on the Continent.

The discourse on the "Moustier Royal" and on Eleanor of Aquitaine has already connected Fontevrault abbey with the pseudo-Map Cycle. It was the administrative capital of the order to which it gave its name, founded in 1099 by Robert d'Abrissel, on Angevin ground but in the diocese of Poitiers. All other houses were priories, and all were responsible, not to bishops, but to the abbess; she depended directly upon the Pope. Among the nuns many were from the noblest French and English families. The birth of the abbess was usually even higher than that of the nuns; fifteen of the first thirty-two abbesses were princesses. The order was by its constitution the natural refuge of devotees of aristocratic romance, not necessarily frivolous romance, for Jacques de Vitry, who was flourishing at the period of interest to us, while condemning the lightness of conduct of noble canonesses, praises the manner of life of the Fontevrists. Thus both the Prose *Lancelot* and the *Queste* might have gained their protection.

Inasmuch as the abbey of Fontevrault was the capital of an order widely distributed, it is appropriate to examine the possibilities of Fontevrist influence beyond the abbey's walls upon the pseudo-Map Cycle. Consideration of its distribution in England may for the moment be postponed. On the Continent its priories were not established in the eastern part of France. In fact they were mainly in the domain of the Angevin kings or on its fringes, except for southwestern Champagne. As might be expected, the concentration was greatest near the mother abbey, in Anjou and northern Poitou. The Breton priories were all in the diocese of Nantes. South of Poitou, even into Languedoc, there were houses, but for the present purposes these may be neglected.

Saumur and Chinon have figured prominently in earlier discussions. The history of the order written by its *religieuses* notes two priories, Montsoreau and Les Loges, as being near Saumur (Fon II.10), the latter founded by 1109 (Fon I.104). The house at Brueil, later called more frequently La Tourette, was "dans les environs de Chinon" (Fon I.134). It was founded before 1117. Earlier in this study, Guesnes, extracted from Monts-sur-Guesnes, was proposed as the altered model for the name Gaunes. An estate presented to the order by 1109 was at "Gaisnes, près de Loudun" (Fon I.106), which correctly describes the location of Monts-sur-Guesnes. The house founded there was the harbor of retirement for Foulques, count of Anjou. Mirebeau, we have seen, was perhaps the site of the last castle held by King Bohort's widow. The Fontevrist order acquired an estate there, named Boissy, before 1117.

The interest that the romance shows in Berry may originate in the desire of Fontevrist religious in the diocese of Bourges where there came to be four of their foundations; of these, the oldest, Orsan, was founded before 1117 (Fon I.121) in the western part of the province at some distance to the southeast of Issoudun and Charost, mentioned in the *Benoic-Gaunes*; also a priory was set up closer to these towns and to the northwest at Jarzay, and another at Longefont to the west.

The puzzling preference for Meaux is perhaps occasioned by Fontevrist interests. Two priories were in the diocese of Meaux, Fontaine-en-France, within five miles of the town, and Collinance, described by the religious as "près La Ferté-Milon à trente-quatre kilomètres de Château-Thierry" (Fon II.11). There were three foundations in the diocese of Rouen and one not far beyond to the south, Chaise-Dieu at L'Aigle, founded in 1132 (Fon II.29). Thus contacts with Richard Marshal during his Norman period may have occurred. There were no Flemish houses, but there were two in Picardy, Mauréancourt in the diocese of Amiens (Fon II.11) and Charmes on the Oise in the diocese of Laon, northwest of Laon toward the towns on the Somme. False Baldwin's collapse at Péronne would have been well known in these monastic houses.

The Plantagenet royal house was repeatedly a protector of Fontevrault abbey. In 1176 at Chinon, Henry II offered the Abbess Audeburge the establishment at Amesbury in England, of which more later. In the 1180s he made it possible for the nuns to stay at Fontevrault when crop failures were about to drive them out (Fon II, 57, 71).

The obituary of Eleanor of Aquitaine inserted into the abbey records, after praising her above all earthly queens, goes on:

Ecclesiae Fontis Ebraldi advocata, nos, pariter ac parentes suos ordinem nostrum ampliori prae ceteris religiosis charitate complectens, redditibus ampliavit, multis et innumeris elleemosynarum ditavit beneficiis [a list follows and the obituary concludes] velamen nostri ordinis suscipere et in nostra praeelegit ecclesia sepeliri. (Quoted on p. 234n by LA from "Arch. de Maine-et-Loire, H non coté, ed. B. Pavillon, La vie du bienheureux Robert d'Abrissel . . . Saumur, 1667, p. 589")

Clearly, and as expected, the affection of Eleanor and the nuns of Fontevrault was mutual. And the abbey sheltered her children. In 1170 Henry and Eleanor placed their son John, then aged four, there for a year, also their daughter Joan, just younger, who remained at the house until she was taken at the age of eleven to become the bride of the king of Naples (Pic 87; K 259). King Richard the Lion-Hearted was generous to the abbey; on his liberation from prison, which the nuns attributed to their prayers, says their obituary of him, "benigne nos visitavit, Ecclesiam nostram quam inter ceteras regni sui praecipuam habebat, reliquis praecipuis dotavit, et honorabit, videlicet ligno crucis Dominico, capillisque Dei genetricis" (Pic 44). His tomb is at Fontevrault by his own direction. Henry III also gave his heart for burial there. On this occasion, the abbey's obituary commented thus upon his generosities to it: "noster progenitor, atquae tutor pronus ex cujus praecordiali et abundante largitione toties nobis dona prae maxima fere inenerrabilia et quasi in estimabilia provenerunt" (Pic 196). During the reigns of King John, Henry III, and in part of Edward I, the abbey of Fontevrault received a regular gift from the English kings originally established for masses for Eleanor at seventy pounds a year, increased to eighty pounds in 1242 by Henry, who also from 1249 paid an annuity to Alice of Blois, qualified as his kinswoman. She was for a short time abbess, later a simple nun. (See Close and Liberate Rolls in Index under "Fontevrault.") Edward I and his sister likewise gave their hearts to the abbey.

After the death of Henry II, the abbey of Fontevrault, without his protection, was in economic distress. The convocation of the general chapter was put off by the Abbess Matilda of Flanders (1189–1194) "tum pro bladi raritate quem habemus, tum pro nimia paupertate quam et nos et vos pariter sustinemus" (Pic 38).

The immediate successors of Matilda are those of greatest interest to us. They were: Mathilde de Bohème, widow of Thibaut, count of

Champagne (1194–1207); Marie de Champagne, daughter of the above, and widow of the duke of Burgundy (1207–1208); Alix de Champagne, granddaughter of Mathilde (1209–1218); Berthe, of unknown origin (1218–1228); and Adèle de Bretagne, of the ducal house (1228–1244).

The connection of the Fontevrists with the ruling house of Champagne may in part explain the interest of the pseudo-Map Cycle in Meaux. The grand prioress under the first of these abbesses was Adèle de Blois, younger than her abbess, energetic, and primarily in charge of the administration of the abbey and the order. Though political events affected Fontevrault in these years, the continued residence of Queen Eleanor at the abbey indicates that under Adèle's guidance the institution prospered. Of these years Colonel Picard remarks, concerning the nuns, "Les unes se firent artistes, d'autres artisons" (Pic 39). He considers such occupations demeaning to ladies of high degree, and, attributing their industry to poverty, calls the nuns, "pauvres dames." I see the activity, rather, as creating an atmosphere favorable to the Cyclic Project.

The situation at Fontevrault seems to have deteriorated in the next administration under Alix, 1209–1218. The *History* by the religious reports much devastation in her time (Fon II.93). Berthe, who succeeded her, "s'appliqua à maintenir le bon ordre et à améliorer la situation critique de son abbaye" (Fon II.100). She was victor in a struggle with neighboring bishops and with part of the male element in the order. Adèle de Bretagne, who became abess in 1228, had been brought up at the English court, took her vows at Amesbury priory at the age of twenty, and resided there for a while before transferring to Fontevrault. As soon as she was installed, she went back to the English house "où l'appelaient des intérêts pressants. . . . Ambresbury était son berceau de prédilection" (Fon II.105). She was in Normandy after her visit to England, and was throughout her career an active and potent personage.

Under the conditions existent at Fontevrault after Eleanor died and Anjou became Capetian in 1204, we may assume that in the mother house at Fontevrault projects undertaken by the queen fell into abeyance. But at Amesbury, the principal Fontevrist house in England, activity in the domain of art could prosper after 1216. And Adèle would have tended to promote an ambitious project nearing its end.

While Lancelot's career began near the site of the abbey of Fontevrault, Arthur's last battle was fought near the site of the priory of Amesbury. The *Mort Artu* groups place names about Amesbury in much the same way as the *Benoic-Gaunes* puts all scenes of action within easy reach of Fontevrault. I have already spoken of the fact that Amesbury is on the eastern edge of the Salisbury Plain. Lot (LEt 196n1) and Frappier (FEt 175n3) accept the identification of the institution at Amesbury with the "almiere de Salebieres," where Bohort's record of the events of the Quest of the Holy Grail are preserved (Q 280). Lot adds: "Aussi, sans doute, le 'grant livre' des 'faitz' de Lancelot trouvé en l' 'aumaire' du roi Arthur après la bataille de Salisbury (V, 191)" (LEt 196n1). He seems on the threshold of making a connection with the Fontevrists. Winchester is not far from the town by the plain (twenty-two miles), and on the way from it to London one reaches the headwaters of the Lodden after some twenty-five miles and Shalford by going about as much farther. The short distances westward to scenes of action in the *Mort Artu* have already received comment. Lot (LEt 195–96), Bruce (BE I.430), and Frappier (FEt 175–76) have puzzled over the reason for locating Arthur's last battle on Salisbury Plain and have maintained the probability that the suggestion for the setting came from a passage in Wace's *Brut*, either directly or by way of Robert de Boron's *Merlin*. In 1155, before the abbey at Amesbury was displaced by the Fontevrist priory, Wace was indeed locating Salisbury Plain by means of the house; his version of the Saxon massacre of the Britons makes it take place

As granz plaines de Salesbire
Lez l'abeie de Ambresbire [W vv. 7227–28]

in the midst of a conference to which Hengist had lured his victims.

These two verses of Wace contain the words "plaines" and "Ambresbire"; Geoffrey of Monmouth employed neither a century before, though he designates the same spot. His account (HRB VI.15) says that the unhappy conference is to take place "juxta coenobium Ambrii," and adds that the burial takes place "haud longe a Kaercaraduc, quae nunc Salesberia dicitur, in cimeterio quod juxta coenobium Ambrii abbatis, qui olim fundator ipsius extiterat." Later the king "ivit ad monasterium prope Kaercaradoc quod nunc Salisberia dicitur, ubi consules ac principes jacebant, quos nefandus Hengistus prodiderat. Erat ibi coenobium trecentorum fratrum in monte Ambrii, qui, ut fertur, fundator ejusdem olim extiterat" (HRB VIII.9).

As a memorial to the murdered nobles, by Merlin's magic the stones for Stonehenge are brought from Ireland. There is a celebration "in monte Ambrii" (HRB VIII.12), after which Merlin sets up the stones. Later Constantine "infra lapidum structuram sepultus fuit quae haud longe a Salesburia mira arte composita. Anglorum lingua Stanheng nuncupatur" (HRB XI.4). Massacre, abbey, and cemetery, all seem created to account for Stonehenge. I suspect, however, that Geoffrey knew the place by reputation rather than from a visit, for to designate the swell in the land on which Stonehenge stands as a "mons" seems unnecessary exaggeration. Certainly, he has no use for nuns in an abbey founded by Saxon Alfrida; his invention of Ambrius and three hundred monks lends dignity to his account. But Wace does not accept his creation. He says that the massacre took place "lez Ambrebiere" (W v. 7741) and has the king go

> a Ambresbiere
> Pur visiter le cimetire
> U cil erent ensepeli
> Ki as cultels furent murdri. (W vv. 7993–96)

And Merlin, after loading his stones in Ireland,

> A Ambresbire les porterent
> En la champaine iluec dejuste. (W vv. 8160–61)

He also identifies them after Merlin erects them as Stonehenge (W v. 8177).

Geoffrey's Latin and Wace's French accounts both bring out how close the spatial association of Amesbury and Salisbury was in popular opinion. When the author of the *Mort Artu* speaks of Salisbury Plain and the *Queste* of the "almiere de Salebieres," we are justified in seeing in their words an allusion to Amesbury.

The mystery of Stonehenge, heightened by folk tales, probably moved Geoffrey to locate episodes there. In the *Mort Artu* the stone setting forth Merlin's prophecy is merely a feature of Salisbury Plain; he wishes to emphasize the general area rather than the prehistoric display. (See further page 135 in the Appendix dealing with the Battle of Salisbury in Robert de Boron's *Merlin*.)

The Fontevrists came to Amesbury in 1177 by the fiat of Henry II, who accused their English predecessors of laxness (which would not be out of harmony with a tendency to harbor *jongleurs*). When Giraldus Cambrensis wrote *De Principis Instructione* nearly twenty years later, he was still indignant at the intrusion of the "transmarinas" (R21 VIII.170). The "transmarinas" were doubtless inclined to carry on the enterprises and interest of their mother house—including a penchant for romances with ideological implications. Wace's allusion suggests that the Amesbury house already had a reputation for literary connections, which might have continued to draw toward the place persons of such tastes.

The nuns imported by Henry II numbered between twenty-one and twenty-four. Some were added from the Fontevrist house at Westwood in Worcestershire. King Henry contributed much to the building of a new house and church in which he and the abbess of Fontevrault installed the nuns in 1186. The presence of male religious is first mentioned in a charter of 1189, and there was a prior in Fontevrault in 1193. In 1256, when the sacristan from Fontevrault went over the accounts, there were a prioress and seventy-six nuns, a prior and six other chaplains, a clerk, and sixteen lay brethren.

Eleanor of Aquitaine, during her period of eclipse and imprisonment, was most frequently near or perhaps in Amesbury, at neighboring Salisbury, or elsewhere in Wiltshire. Geoffrey of Vigeois says, "[Rex] conjugem propriam, matrem filiorum, apud Angliam in turre de Saliberi per plures annos inclusit" (HGF XII.443). In 1174, 1175, and 1176 the Pipe Rolls show items granted her keepers for her maintenance in Wiltshire without specifying where in the county (Ey 180, 197). In Eyton's record for the year 1180, he remarks, "Queen Eleanor ... was probably a prisoner all this time at one of the King's Wiltshire residences," and quotes from the Pipe Roll of that year (Ey 231). When she was outside of Wiltshire, the grants were most frequently made for neighboring areas; upkeep grants were repeatedly made for Winchester (Ey 197, 206, 275), for Dorset and Somerset shires (Ey 241, 247, 280), and for Berkshire (Ey 247). The records show that from 1183 through 1186 the queen was rather frequently with the king, so that we may suppose that she was in his company during the ceremonies at Amesbury in 1186. Thus it is probable that Eleanor was as well acquainted with the Fontevrist priory at Amesbury as she was with the mother abbey. Evidence that her attentions to the English house did not end with her years under surveillance also exists. Just released from prison by Henry's death, the queen in 1189 "gave 20 marks for her late husband's soul" (WH III.245). In 1199 she confirmed a gift of land, half of Winterslow Manor, to Amesbury priory, which was made by her "domicilla et nutrita" Amiria upon entering the convent. This Amiria or Amaria appears also as attendant upon Eleanor when in 1184, during the period of less severe captivity, the queen was allowed to go to Winchester to see her daughter Matilda (R49 I.313). Although Amy Kelly qualifies her as the queen's "maid" (K 191), "lady in waiting" seems more appropriate, for she was of sufficient importance to be outfitted at the same time as Eleanor through a royal grant. She was the sister of Hugh Pantulph, a gentleman holding lands in Shropshire, specified in 1212–1214 as "uadleto" of the king (PPR 86, 91). "Valet," like "domicilla," implies more dignity than the modern term expresses. The Red Book of the Exchequer between 1194 and 1212 shows him owing to the king the services of two to six "milites" in Shropshire, some also in Staffordshire (R99 Index). In 1212 the Book of Fees calls him "baro." He owed service for five "militum" (BF 144). "In 1203 the prioress was made the channel for paying to the Abbess of Fonte-vrault a rent out of the Exchequer for the support of the chaplain praying for the health of Eleanor of Aquitaine's soul" (WH III.245). We know the names of two women who were prioresses in the period of interest to us, Emelina (Emeline) and Felicia (Felise); the name of the former appears in acts of 1208, 1211, and 1221 (WH III.258; and CF 37), of the latter in acts of 1227 and 1237 (idem). Unfortunately we have no further information on them. John de Vinci was prior in 1227 and is likely the same John as he who is recorded in 1215, 1220, and 1221. Henry III "visited Amesbury in 1223, 1231, 1241, and 1256" and showed his liberality a number of times. "Before 1233 Alpesia, the King's cousin, had been admitted as a nun" (LR I.195, 12 Jan. 1233). In 1236 and 1239 the king confirmed privileges and grants made by charters "predecessorum nostrorum regum Anglie" (ClR IV.159; and III.405). "In 1241 Eleanor of Brittany [Henry III's cousin] . . . be-queathed her body to Amesbury."[5] There were other gifts to com-

---

[5] Eleanor of Brittany ended her life as a nun at Bristol. As the child of King John's older brother, Geoffrey, she could claim to be the rightful heir to the throne of England after her brother Arthur's death. She was therefore long a prisoner of John's and of Henry III's in his minority. She was in Corfe Castle in 1221 when William Marshal and William Longsword (her uncle) along with Hubert de Burgh and William Brewer took possession of the fortress (NH 169). Its keeper, Peter de Maulay, had been accused of plotting to deliver her to the king of France (NH 179). Her life was so obscure that no reminiscences of it would be awakened in the public by the vague likeness of her fate to the last days of Guenevere in the Mort Artu; but her connections with Amesbury, William Marshal, and William Longsword arouse a suspicion that perhaps the author sometimes thought of her as he wrote of a queen shut up twice in a castle, buffeted by changing political winds, finally achieving peace as a religious.

memorate the Breton descendants of Henry II and Eleanor. Adèle de Bretagne, their relative, was, as we have seen, a nun at Amesbury, with her loyalty enduring after she became abbess of Fontevrault. Eleanor of Provence, widow of Henry III, passed her last days at the priory; we may assume that her connections were established early, since she was so pious as to have been sainted. Mary, the sixth daughter of Edward I, entered the priory in 1285 and spent her life there. The manner of living of some others there was probably similar to Mary's; according to R. B. Pugh, whose source is here Mary E. Green's *Lives of the Princesses of England*, her life was "spiritually unedifying, devoted, as it was, to travel, junketing, and dicing" (WH III.247).[6] The constant relations between the priory and the mother house are also evident from the royal data. The close connection of Amesbury priory with the royal family may be considered an example of the nuns' general aristocratic background. Amesbury, like Fontevrault, was a proper breeding ground for tales suited to the nobility.

The connection of Amesbury with matters Arthurian became a tradition. The Stanzaic *Morte Arthure* and Sir Thomas Malory locate Guenevere's last retreat at Amesbury. According to the former the queen went "To Amysbery a nonne hyr to make" (MAS v. 3569). Malory is still more specific. Guenevere, after learning of the deaths on Salisbury Plain, "stale away with fyve ladyes with her, and so she went to Amysbyry. And there she lete make herselff a nunne, and wered whyght clothys and blak" (Vin 1243.3-6). The garments here described are the habit of Fontevrist nuns. By the fourteenth century the French source of the English romances had settled on Amesbury as Guenevere's last retreat.

---

[6] Pugh is summarizing from Volume II of Mary Anne Everett Green's *Lives of the Princesses of England* (London 1849); here are Mrs. Green's words on the subject:

"Were we, however, to associate with her [the princess's] future existence [after taking the veil] the ideas of complete disruption of all earthly ties, the perpetual banishment from society, and the weary confinement to a single solitary spot of ground . . . we should greatly err" (p. 411).

"Her bed was hung with velvet and tapestry, and furnished with the finest linen . . . . Her favorite article of diet seems to have been fish, and of this the king frequently presented her with considerable quantities: in one year alone he sent her sixteen sea-wolves to Amesbury . . . . The other princesses were content to travel with one or two chariots and six or at most eight horses; but when the Lady Mary made her appearance at court, it was with a train of twenty-four horses, each of which had a groom in attendance, beside the sumpterers who had charge of the luggage . . . . The pecuniary embarrassments of the princess were owing, however, less to her extravagant personal expenditure . . . than to a love of gambling" (p. 423).

Our only record of relations of Amesbury priory with William Longsword is in royal directives to the sheriff of Wiltshire. During twenty of the years between 1199 and 1226 William Longsword was sheriff (WH V.6–7). In 1206, King John, addressing William as both sheriff and earl, required him to cause to be delivered to the prioress of Amesbury eighteen pounds bound up in dealings going back to the year in which Queen Eleanor, his mother, died (1204). On the sixth of October, 1216, Henry III (his regency, necessarily) directs the sheriff of Wiltshire to have the prioress of Amesbury return to his mother, Isabelle of Angoulême, any money taken from the manor of "Wintrelewe," which was part of Isabelle's dowery.[7]

Longsword's widow evidently thought the atmosphere at Amesbury too worldly. Instead of entering the priory in the town in which she had been born, she founded a nunnery of her own not far-off at Lacock. She had hoped to make this institution Cistercian, but had to content herself with the Augustinian dispensation. Her enthusiasm for Cistercians may have been a link between the Cyclic Project and the author of the *Queste* by way of Longsword and the Marshals. Though there are no official documents to show relations between the Marshal family and Amesbury, the passage in the *Queste* on the "almiere" may contain a witness to such relations. It reads: "Quant Boorz ot contees les aventures del Seint Graal telles come il les avoit veues, si furent mises en escrit et gardees en l'almiere de Salebieres" (Q 279.32–280.1). Since I believe Bohort to be a figure of Richard Marshal, I see in this passage a method of saying that Richard Marshal brought the Grail story to Amesbury.

If the relations between Amesbury and the authors of the Prose *Lancelot* were close, we may ask whether other Fontevrist houses in England furnished background. According to Chettle there were only three other houses, those at Nuneaton, Westwood, and Leighton-Buzzard, otherwise called Grovebury.[8] The last was inhabited by men

---

[7] The manor of "Wintrelewe" was presumably Winterslow. By the act of Eleanor already cited, which confirms Amiria's gift, it was half in the priory's possession. The Fontevrists must have been enjoying the whole income during the period of Isabelle's disgrace. Isabelle was doubtless making her claim because Winterslow was part of Eleanor's dower lands and those lands had become part of her own dowery. Isabelle was unwilling apparently to accept the alienation which had, it seems, gone through two steps: Eleanor to Amiria, then Amiria to the priory. If Eleanor had not held the manor first, her confirmation of Amiria's gift would hardly have been necessary.

[8] The *History* by the Fontevrist religious lists six English houses (Fon II.12). Westwood appears as "Wertwode," Grovebury as "Gravbury," Nuneaton as "Etonne." "Lar-

who, according to Chettle, were the "business managers of the order in England" (CF 37). The chief proof of this function, at least for the thirteenth century, seems to be that from 1227 to 1240 the Liberate Rolls ordered that the grant to the abbey of Fontevrault be consigned for transmittal to the prior of Leighton (later to the prior of La Grave in the territory on the Continent still possessed by the English kings). Their contacts with the abbey in France would therefore have been frequent, but there is only one hint in the pseudo-Map Cycle to implicate them in the fabrication of the romance. Leighton-Buzzard, some thirty-five air miles north-northwest of London, may possibly be on the site of the castle named Lamborc in the *Mort Artu* (108.6). Arthur and his forces at war with Lancelot leave Kamaalot for Joyous Guard and reach Lamborc at the end of the first day. "El l'endemain firent ausi grant jornee comme il avoient fet le jor devant" (108.6–8). A long day's march from Westminster might end at Leighton, which lies in the direction from the capital to be taken on a journey toward a castle on the Humber. The name "Lamborc" could have been invented by using parts of Leighton and Grovebury ("borc" and "bury" have the same etymon). It is rather strange that this castle name should be specified and none other on the way to Joyous Guard.

Nuneaton and Westwood may be investigated as lying on the road from Kamaalot to Taneborc-Oswestry. Nothing in the *Mort Artu* hints at Nuneaton, but Westwood may have been the inspiration for situating Morgan's castle. Westwood lies some fifty-five miles south-west of Oswestry. Westwood priory, says Chettle, "lay a few miles west of Droitwich and the Bromsgrove-Worcester road, 'in a vast and solitary wood' but close to a lake" (CF 36). King Arthur, leaving Taneborc, journeyed one day to Tauroc, stayed there three days, and leaving it, "il erra jusqu'a un bois . . . si forvoierent tant qu'il perdirent lor droit chemin del tout en tout" (48.8–16). Fortunately, they found a rich abode, that of Arthur's sister Morgan, as shelter for the night. Morgan's castle resembled no nunnery, and castles in the midst of forests are commonplaces in romances, but the distances as well as the surroundings are right. If we grant that the aged Queen Eleanor, the Marshals, and the Fontevrist nuns were patrons of the pseudo-Map Cycle, it becomes evident why conventional morality necessarily tri-

---

grave" is possibly a deformation of Leighton, repeating Grovebury. I have no guess as to the identity of "Heibvok." Chettle's article is completely documented, and for England is to be preferred to the record of the religious.

umphs at its end: a woman approaching death and members of a religious order would give the negative the advantage in a debate on the value of courtly love.

Much earlier in this study I commented on the appropriateness of the choice of Meaux as a town just beyond the boundaries of the Ile de France suitable for the recovery of wounded Gawain in the *Mort Artu*. I did not emphasize, however, how exactly the author was acquainted with the provincial boundary and what care he took to name the town. The author of the *Estoire* went much farther out of his way when he wrote: "Tu [Evalac] fus nes a vne anchiene cyte qui est apelee meau[l]s en france" (I.47.11–12). He specifies France and not Gaul for the greater geographic unit—which is bizarre for an event occurring at the very beginning of the Christian era. The man who wrote the *Estoire* could not be the same as the author of the *Mort Artu* (their styles are poles apart), and the fact that both name Meaux seems evidence that a preliminary sketch of the pseudo-Map Cycle outlined its entirety; in this the town must have been specified. Someone who held the town dear must have desired greatly to see it commemorated, a noble nun at Fontevrault perhaps. Whoever the person was, she or he influenced details widely separated in the Cycle.

As we have seen, the hypothesis under consideration assumes that the composition of the pseudo-Map Cycle falls into three periods: an early period extending from 1194 or 1196 to 1202 or 1204, the last years of the life of Queen Eleanor; a main period, running from 1217 or 1222 to the mid 1230s; and a late period, continuing on until about 1246, date of the death of Isabelle of Angoulême. Though scholars differ as to the dating of the Cycle, they agree that the romances of the late period, the *Merlin* Continuations, were written later than the rest of it (see, for instance, A 295, 322). They also agree that composition took place in the thirteenth century. Thus, only the notion of an early period is an innovation on my part. For brevity the following description of the characteristics of each period is couched in absolute terms, but with full consciousness that many affirmations are speculative.

In the early period the Cyclic Plan was laid out, including the main divisions and such specifications as that Lancelot should be buried at the scene of his first great exploit, that he should recover his lost kingdom, and that Mordred should be rejected by a skilled Guenevere. Other specifications of minor importance included such items as mentions of Meaux to suit some enthusiast for the region. The *Benoic-Gaunes* and probably all the *Galehaut* were planned in some detail.

The *Mort Ban* was written in the form finally preserved, the planning and the writing being done at Fontevrault or nearby.

Near the beginning of the main period the Cyclic Plan was revised, sometimes importantly, for instance, in introducing mysticism and a demonstration of the folly of vendettas, changes strengthening the case of the negative. The plan as then formed therefore included a Galahad who could become the perfect mystic, and a Gawain who thirsted after vengeance. The development of the technique of narrative intertwinements, which has its germ in the *Mort Ban* where the siege of Banin is sandwiched into the story of the rape of Lancelot, requires the projection of the course of many narrative threads without the elaboration of adventures strung along the threads.

What I have said concerning geography and varying political prejudices implies that composition went on at points in England and on the Continent sometimes quite distant from one another. As a consequence it is difficult to tell which sections were written before certain others. The *Claudas-Frolle* might have been written before the *Mort Artu*, or after it. Neither shows the influence of the other, only that of the sometimes imperfectly interpreted specifications of the Cyclic Plan.

The Cycle was probably assembled in England, seat of the patrons. A bit of evidence in support of this view is found in the "almiere" passage. If Richard Marshal (Bohort) brought the story of the Grail adventures to Amesbury priory (the "almiere") "dont Mestre Gautier Map les trest a fere son livre" (Q 280.1–2), the implication is that Amesbury was the place of revision and assembly. Possibly also, the words "por l'amor del roi Henri son seignor" mean that the Marshals intended to present the Cycle to Henry III, the brother-in-law of William Marshal, Jr.

In the late period, Robert's *Merlin* (which I suspect was undertaken for this project in the early period; see the Appendix) became the point of departure for its Continuations, written in the Poitevin region.

The writers who worked out the narratives within the Cyclic Plan may sometimes be distinguished from one another. I now expand hints that I have given concerning them. I believe that we may distinguish:

1. An author of the *Estoire*;

2. authors of the *Merlin* Continuations working late but under Fontevrist and Poitevin influence;

3. an author for the *Mort Ban*, practically, Eleanor of Aquitaine;

4. an author of the *Benoic-Gaunes*, well versed in Plantagenet and Poitevin affairs, especially concerned with the borderlands between Anjou and Poitou, displaying no knowledge of British topography;

5. an author for the *False Guenevere*, likely a Fleming or Picard; unlike the author of the *Mort Artu*, he treats Arthur without sympathy;

6. an author of the *Claudas-Frolle*, with Capetian sympathies, but none for Thibaut of Champagne;

7. an author of the *Queste*;

8. an author of the *Mort Artu*, a lover of England, perhaps not one of its natives, but uninterested in Anjou and Poitou.

Because of the political preoccupations common to the authors of the *Benoic-Gaunes* and the *Mort Artu* and the similarity of their techniques in handling place-names, there is a temptation to identify them as the same man; but the treatment that they give geography precludes this view. They must have exchanged opinions on theoretical matters and been closely bound to the patrons, but neither could have traveled much through the settings of the other's romance.

I incline to think that the *Galehaut*, after the first 118 pages of Volume III, was written by one man, different from the author of the *Benoic-Gaunes*, but that to the end of the capture of Dolorous Guard he was controlled by the details of the early plan. He may have extended his work through some passages of Volume IV, but he did not write the *False Guenevere*, where political interests are so important. I doubt that he wrote the Grail passages, though he may have inserted them into the matrix; at most, he, a member of the affirmative, composed these according to specifications furnished by the negative.

When the actors of the *Benoic-Gaunes* reenter the romance, I sense that another author, not the author of the *Benoic-Gaunes* and not the writer of the *Galehaut*, is at work and probably has been for some time. This man appears not to have known the *Benoic-Gaunes* in its finished form, but to have depended upon the section devoted to it in the main period plan.

In Volume V the number of authors seems great. They are often, though not always, ignorant of or indifferent to what others had written; and sometimes, though not always, restive under the specifications set up for them. For the most part they are more interested in telling a tale than expounding an ideology.

The structure of the *Queste* and the *Estoire* lead me to speculate as follows: Two men were assigned as collaborators to work out the details of the romances in accordance with the Cyclic Plan as revised in the main period. They prepared a scenario more complete than that in the plan and together wrote out the passages common to both romances. Then they separated and each completed his romance in accordance with his personality. Thus we can understand why the passages appearing in both romances harmonize stylistically and ideologically, whereas except in these passages the style and ideas of each work seem radically different from those of the other. Such a conclusion from the available facts explains more ambiguities than other guesses (for bibliography, see C 10).

The author of the *Mort Artu* knew the *Queste* in a way, but he paid such small attention to it as to lead one to believe that he had not read the completed work, was acquainted only with the detailed plan for it. Something similar seems true as regards his knowledge of the castle of Joyous Guard and of the foreshadowings in the *Agravain*.

The hypothetical history of the writing of the pseudo-Map Cycle set down above can never be proved in its entirety, but it presents a harmonious explanation of phenomena that have perplexed many scholars and have sometimes led to affirmations far more hazardous than any ventured above as probable. The value of this hypothetical history lies not only in its dates and its naming of places and people, of kings, queens, and great lords, but especially in explaining the genesis of a work of great diversity of character but valuable as an entity. Without the concept of cyclic unity great passages are much diminished in interest and in meaning. For instance, if we remember the total intent of the authors, we may realize that Lancelot's last grieving hours at the castle of Joyous Guard when the best knight in the world gave up the woman who had so long been his reason for existence are not only an antithesis to the proud elated moments when he turned Dolorous Guard into Joyous Guard, but also the final exposition in the *Mort Artu* of the futility of the whole course of courtly love; then the irony of those few pages cuts deeper. An understanding of the timeliness of the Cycle may provide like recognitions. Knowing that the deaths of Ban and Henry II were much alike should increase the sense of the futility of human endeavor that each of those deaths may evoke. A similar increase in perception of futility should be aroused by recognizing that Louis's rush across southern England after fleeing John eventually helped him no more than the precipitous march of Arthur and Mordred across the same country to be killed on Salisbury Plain.

Appendix

A Hypothesis on the Relation of Outside Grail Romances to the Pseudo-Map Cycle

The relation of the *Perlesvaus* and the works of Robert de Boron to the pseudo-Map Cycle was, as I surmise, of the following nature. When the Cycle was planned, the divisions laid out were roughly those eventually developed, but did not include the reformation of Lancelot nor the creation of Galahad. When sections were assigned for composition in the early period, Robert de Boron received the commission to do both the early history of the Grail and the *enfances* of Arthur, the latter to begin with a *Merlin*.

The commission for the late Grail romance fell to a man who, like all the original planners, was faithful to Perceval, but who enjoyed play on words and insisted that his Grail family should have names revealing allegorical significance. Thus the Fisher King should be called Messios (Messiah), and his sister, Iglais (Eglise). The Grail hero should be called something showing his divine origin, and the author suggested that he be called Par-lui-fet "por ce qu'il s'estoit fet par lui meïsmes" (2931–32). When the Cyclic planners objected, he agreed to making that form of the name simply a soubriquet invented by the hermit king. He held out, however, for an appellation revealing more evidently than Per(d)-ce-val that the Grail achiever was the son of man, participating in mankind's fallen state; that is, he made the planners accept Per(d)-les-vaus. An early version of the passage in Sommer, III.29, was written using this name.

When the death of Eleanor ended the early period, Robert de Boron went ahead with his assignment under other sponsorship. So also did he who had insisted on "Perlesvaus." Possibly, too, disapproving of the *Perlesvaus* upon its appearance and seeing no prospect of a *Mort Artu*, Robert wrote or persuaded another to write the Didot-*Perceval* (on which see further below).

When the Cyclic Plan was overhauled at resumption of the project in

133

the main period, Robert de Boron had finished his production, and the *Perlesvaus*[1] had been written. The revisers, as I guess their motivations, while accepting the *Merlin*, rejected the Grail romances (Robert's *Joseph* and the *Perlesvaus*) for these reasons among others:

1. The *Joseph* and the *Perlesvaus* did not allow enough generations between the time of Christ and that of Arthur;

2. the *Joseph* slighted conversions to Christianity;

3. it ignored an ancestry for Lancelot;

4. the *Perlesvaus* damned Lancelot, all the while exalting his character (C 28);

5. Perlesvaus was objectionably bloodthirsty (the original Perceval was also not ideal because *nice* and subject to too many human failings);

6. the *Perlesvaus* killed Guenevere (and the Didot-*Perceval*, if already written, ignored her).

Even under the original plan not all these flaws were excusable. While Wace and Geoffrey's data might be altered, there was no intention of destroying a few hundred years of history that they had invented. No one had ever intended damnation for Lancelot and Guenevere, nor to do away with the queen before the end of the Cycle.

The revision of the plan remedied all this, and added much. The invention of Galahad was an important innovation. Because of it instructions were given to alter the passage in III.29 to suit the new concepts, but the author of the *Benoic-Gaunes,* as a member of the affirmative team, was not greatly interested in this new hero of the negative and botched the job, making additions without changing names. Possibly, while remembering that the Grail hero was to be a bastard, he still confused the circumstances of his conception with the incestuous origin arranged for Mordred, with the result that in calling Amide both mother and sister he meant what he said. Probably the affirmative had conceded incest by Arthur in return for the negative's letting Lancelot, the faithful courtly lover, engender Galahad without betraying Guenevere. Thus the two phenomena of illegitimacy were linked in the mind of the author of the *Benoic-Gaunes*.

The ideological and chronological features of the above hypothesis explain four matters:

1. The passage in Sommer, III.29;

2. how Robert's *Joseph*, the Cyclic *Estoire,* and the *Perlesvaus* all three at points harmonize and at others contradict one another, expounding nearly the same origin for the Grail, but differing in many features concerning the Grail family;

---

[1] J. Neale Carman, "South Welsh Geography and British History in the *Perlesvaus*," appearing in *A Medieval French Miscellany* (Lawrence: University of Kansas Publications, 1972), edited by Norris J. Lacy, treats problems similar to those investigated in the first five chapters of this study as does *Res. Stud.*, 32 (1964), 85–105.

3. certain characteristics of the *Queste* and *Mort Artu* that seem *ripostes* to the *Perlesvaus*; for instance, the creation of a peaceable Grail hero *(Queste)*, propaganda against feuds (MA), and the salvation of Lancelot (twice) and of Guenevere (MA);

4. why the Cycle accepted the *Merlin* as a constituent element.

I am inclined to see the influence of the early Cyclic Plan in the *Merlin* account of the Battle of Salisbury, which was fought by Uther and Pendragon against the Saxons (II.49 ff.). Though the *Merlin* here ignores Stonehenge, there may be influences from the Geoffrey-Wace story of operations in the same area of England. But Robert de Boron did not derive from his predecessors the notion of a pitched battle, certainly not one so important as to make Merlin say: "puis que sainte crestiente fu establie en ceste ille not mais si grant bataille ne naura en nos tans com ceste sera" (II.50.3–4). Bruce regarded these pages in the *Merlin* as leading the author of the *Mort Artu* to place Arthur's last battle on Salisbury Plain. Except for the location, however, the combats are as different as two great pitched battles could be. Some more urgent force, such as the pressure of patrons, must have made the author of the *Mort Artu* abandon the tradition furnished by the fictional chronicles for the last battle of Arthur.

The early Cyclic Plan at Fontevrist suggestion presumably specified that Arthur should receive his fatal wound on Salisbury Plain, and that there should be a battle there earlier to make the site more natural; both should be prophesied by Merlin. I hypothesize that Robert was carrying out the plan. Since his battle must seem less important, he exalted it not only by the statement quoted above but also by emphasizing the prophetic element. His whole account of the Salisbury campaign is permeated with Merlin's prophecies. The lines on the battle are few.

Robert insists upon the location, but the geography of his account is at once rather detailed and also rather vague. The Saxons land at some unspecified point and proceed, apparently as marauders, to Salisbury Plain. Uther gathers his forces somewhere on the Thames, marches to the plain, and harasses and immobilizes the Saxons there till they run out of water and come out for battle. Reinforcements under Pendragon have come up, and the Britons win a victory in which Pendragon is killed. Robert seems not well acquainted with the scene himself and is blurring data supplied by someone knowledgeable.

A corollary to the hypothesis on Robert's work is that he wrote his prose versions before his verse. Perhaps we have only a fragment of the verse *Merlin*, not merely because a manuscript is incomplete but also because versification of the prose original written for Eleanor's Cycle is incomplete—it was never finished.

The corollary demands that Robert should have been under the influence of Eleanor of Aquitaine while inditing his prose. If so, we should expect an attitude toward women in the prose *Joseph* different from that in the verse version. Let us consider two bits from the passage in the *Joseph* in which Christ explains the fall of man (for the prose text, Roach's in *RP*, IX [1956], 320–21; for the verse, Nitze's in *Le Roman de l'Estoire dou Graal, CFMA*, 1927, pp. 26–27); here is the first bit:

Prose	Verse
Li Anemis l'engigna	[Adam caused the damnation of man.]
[Eve] et li fist pecier, et	Par la pome que il menja
ele fist pecier Adan. (ll.	Qu'Eve sa fame li donna
225–26)	Par le conseil de l'Ennemi
	Qu'ele plus tost que Dieu creï. (vv. 749–52)

The prose in this passage gives more emphasis to Eve as an actor than the verse. The prose makes her, rather than Adam, responsibe for damnation; in the verse she is hardly more than a channel from the devil to Adam, who is the responsible individual. Eve is deceived, but she is strong in the prose, weak and hesitating in the verse. The prose does not mention her sex; she acts on a par with Adam. The verse calls her "fame" and makes her a seducer. (The influences deduced from this passage could also be based on an earlier one, prose 16–17, verse 84–88.)

Here is the second bit:

Prose	Verse
Nasqui de feme par ce	. . . li Fiuz naschi de la mere.
que par feme avoit por-	Par fame estoit hons adirez,
chachié li Anemis qu'il	Et par fame fu recouvrez;
eüst les homes et tout	Fame la mort nous pourchaca,
aussi comme par feme	Fame vie nous restora;
estoit l'ame de lui en	Par fame estions emprisonné,
prison, covenoit il par	Par fame fumes recouvré. (vv. 762–68)
force qu'ele fust racre-	
antee et rayesse par	
feme. (ll. 228–31)	

In this case both versions treat woman generically; her sex is emphasized. However, the insistence is less in the prose than in the verse; after the intial statement the word "fame" occurs six times in the verse passage, thrice in the prose. The verse by three antitheses portrays woman as an instrument—an instrument of damnation and salvation. She is not a person, but a means, a poison and a panacea. In the prose, woman is a person; the element of her responsibility is almost as evident as in the first passage. Subject only to supernatural forces, the devil, and God, she disposes of men's souls. The soul does not appear in the verse. In the prose it is an entity that woman can cherish, in some sort her child. Finally, whereas in the verse the author seems concerned only with the brilliance of his antithesis, in the prose the phrase "covenoit il par force" seems an assertion that woman's rôle in salvation was an act of justice toward her after she had been overly blamed because the devil had happened to approach her first.

The prose version is at once more sympathetic toward woman and more willing to endow her with strength and personality. Such should be a version created for Eleanor of Aquitaine, while the verse seems made for those to whom woman is an impenetrable mystery. The Didot-*Perceval*, I agree, is a third member of a trilogy (or, if you like, the last two members of a tetralogy), completed, if not by Robert de Boron, by a continuator or adapter who likely had had some communication with Robert. Robert would regret the rôles of Lancelot and Guenevere, but would otherwise follow out the sketch of the Cycle that I have postulated. In passing the matter on to another, he would keep silence on the parts of the Cyclic Plan of which he disapproved. The Didot-*Perceval*, despite others to the contrary, chiefly Pauphilet (Pa 212–17), in my opinion contains nothing that need be regarded as influencing the composition of the pseudo-Map Cycle. I find in all features that the *Mort Artu* and the Didot-*Perceval* have in common nothing that could not have been drawn from Geoffrey's *Historia Regum Britanniae* or from Wace or another translator. Besides the Grail itself, for which there are other sources, the only important feature that the *Queste* and the Didot-*Perceval* both use is the Siege Perilous. Robert's *Joseph* is a sufficient source for both, though I believe that the motif was in the original Cyclic sketch.

Since I regard the pseudo-Map Cycle and the Didot-*Perceval* as independent of each other except in their roots, the dating and authorship of the latter does not concern the present study. For discussion and bibliography see William Roach's edition of the Romance (pp. 113 ff.) and *Arthurian Literature in the Middle Ages* (A 259–60). Lot has the best comments on geographical and historical allusions (LEt 183–85) in the Death of Arthur section, but more words might be devoted to the subject.

Bibliography

Each item of the bibliography is preceded by a siglum, which is used in referring to the work in the text of this volume. The siglum R plus an arabic numeral indicates an item in the Rolls Series; see under Rolls. Similarly, HGF stands for the Bouquet collection; see under *Historiens*.

HGF Albéric des Trois-Fontaines. *Ex Chronico*, HGF XVIII, 744–96. See *Historiens*.

A *Arthurian Literature of the Middle Ages,* Ed. R. S. Loomis. Oxford, 1961.

R49 Benedict of Peterborough. See *Gesta Henrici*.

BF *Book of Fees*, Part I, London, 1920.

HGF Bouquet. See *Historiens*.

BoC Boussard, Jacques. *Le Comté d'Anjou sous Henri Plantagenêt et ses fils, 1151–1204. Bibliothèque de l'Ecole des Hautes Etudes*, no. 271. Paris, 1938.

BoH Boussard, Jacques. *Le Gouvernement d'Henri II Plantagenêt*. Paris, 1956.

BM Boutemy, A. *Gautier Map, conteur anglais*. Brussels, 1945.

BE Bruce, Jas. Douglas. *The Evolution of Arthurian Romance*. 2 vols., second edition. Baltimore, 1928.

MAS Bruce, Jas. Douglas, ed. of Stanzaic *Morte Arthure*. See *Morte*.

Calendar. See *Fine, Inquisitions, Liberate, Patent*.

C Carman, J. Neale. *The Relationship of the Perlesvaus and the Queste del Saint Graal*. University of Kansas Humanistic Studies, Vol. V, No. 4, Lawrence, Kansas, 1936.

CF Chettle, H. F. "The English Houses of the Order of Fontevraud." *Downside Review*, Jan. 1942, 33–55.

Chronicles. See particularly Rolls Series and *Historiens*.

HGF *Chroniques de Saint-Denis*, HGF, XVII, 348–422. See *Historiens*.

ClR   *Close Rolls of the Reigns of John and Henry III*, Vols. I–IV (1204–1242). Public Records Office, London, 1833–1911.

R66   Coggeshall. See Ralph.

CRR   *Curia Regis Rolls*, Vols. III and VI. Public Records Office, London, 1926 and 1932.

HGF   Delisle, L. See *Historiens*.

R68   Diceto. See Ralph.

DP   *The Didot-Perceval*. Ed. William Roach. Philadelphia, 1941.

Ey   Eyton, Robert W. *Court, Household & Itinerary of King Henry II*. London, 1878.

FR   *Fine Rolls, Calendar of the*, Vol. 1 (1272–1307). Public Records Office, London, 1911.

Fon   Fontevrault, Religieuses de Sainte-Marie de. *Histoire de l'ordre de Fontevrault (1100–1908)*. Three volumes. Auch, 1911–1915.*

Fo   Fox, Marjorie B. *La Mort le Roi Artu, Etude*. Paris, 1933.

FEt   Frappier, Jean. *Etude sur la Mort le Roi Artu*. Second edition, Paris, 1961.

FBs   Frappier, Jean. "La Bataille de Salebieres," *Mélanges offertes à Rita Lejeune*. Gembloux: Duculot, 1969, pp. 1007–23.

MA   Frappier, Jean, ed. of *La Mort le roi Artu*, q.v.

ZRP   Freymond, E. "Zum *livre d'Artus*," *Zeitschrift für romanische Philologie*, XVI (1892), 90–127.

Ga   Gallais, Pierre, "Bleheri, la cour de Poitiers et la diffusion des récits arturiens sur le continent," *Moyen Age et Littérature comparée, Actes du VIIᵉ Congrès national de littérature comparée*, Paris, 1967.

HRB   Geoffrey of Monmouth. *Historia regum Britanniae*. Ed. Acton Griscom. New York, 1929.

---

* In this study no citations have been made from *l'Histoire de l'ordre de Font-Evraud* by H. Nicquet, Paris, 1642. The *religieuses* who wrote their history later were evidently familiar with his work, for their plan is very similar to his. The two histories do not contradict each other, and all data which Nicquet presents are included in the work of the *religieuses*. While the latter are all too sparing of documentation, they utilize sources that Nicquet neglected and add many items to the information that he conveyed. He, for instance, speaks of no priories, only of the mother house, and does not, as the *religieuses* do (Fon II.105), cite the connection of Abbess Adèle de Bretagne with Amesbury.

HGF — Geoffroi de Vigeois. *Chronicon Lemovicensis,* HGF, XII, 421–51, XVIII, 211–23. See *Historiens.*

R49 — *Gesta Regis Henrici Secundi Benedicti Abbatis.* Ed. Wm. Stubbs. Two parts, R49, London, 1867. See Rolls.

R21 — *Giraldus Cambrensis* (Gerald of Barry), *The Works of.* Eds. Brewer, Dimock, Warner. Eight parts, R21, London, 1861–1891. See Rolls.

GM — *Guillaume le Maréchal, Histoire de.* Ed. Paul Meyer. Three vols. Paris, 1891–1901.

Hel — Helinand of Froidmont. *Chronicon.* In *Patrologia latina.* Ed. J. P. Migne, Vol. 212, Cols. 771–1082. Paris, 1855.

HNA — *Histoire des ducs de Normandie et des Rois d'Angleterre.* Ed. Francisque Michel. Paris, 1840.

HRB — *Historia Regum Britanniae.* See Geoffrey.

HGF — *Historiens des Gaules et de la France, Recueil des,* Vols. XVII–XVIII, Ed. Léopold Delisle, 1878–1879. See Albéric, Geoffroi, *Chroniques de St. Denis.*

R51 — Hoveden. See Roger.

Ipm — *Inquisitions post mortem, Calendar of the,* Vols. I and II. Public Records Office, London, 1904–1906.

Imc — *Inquisitions miscellaneous (chancery), Calendar of the,* Vol. I. Public Record Office, London, 1916.

R38 — *Itinerarium Peregrinorum et gesta Regis Ricardi.* Ed. Wm. Stubbs. R38, I, London, 1864. See Rolls.

K — Kelly, Amy. *Eleanor of Aquitaine and the Four Kings.* London, 1952.

Ken — Kennedy, Elspeth. "Social and Political Ideas in the French Prose *Lancelot,*" *Medium Aevum,* XXVI (1957), 90–106.

LA — Labande, Edmond René. "Pour une Image véridique d'Aliénor d'Aquitaine," *Bulletin de la Société des antiquaires de l'Ouest et des Musées de Poitiers,* fourth series, II (1952), 175-233.

Lj — Lejeune, Rita. "Rôle littéraire d'Aliénor d'Aquitaine et de sa famille, I. Aliénor," *Cultura Neolatina,* XIV (1954), 5–53. No citations of her "Rôle littéraire de la famille d'Aliénor d'Aquitaine," *Cahiers de civilisation médiévale,* I (1958), 319-37.

LR — *Liberate Rolls, Calendar of the,* Vols. 1–V (1226–1267). Public Records Office, London, 1916–1961.

A   Loomis, R. S. See *Arthurian Literature in the Middle Ages.*

LEt   Lot, Ferdinand. *Etude sur le Lancelot en Prose.* Paris, 1918.

R37   *Magna Vita S. Hugonis episcopi Lincolniensis.* Ed. J. F. Dimock. R37, London, 1856. See Rolls.

Vin   *Malory, Works of Sir Thomas* [commonly called *Morte Darthur*], Ed. Eugene Vinaver. Second edition, three vols., one pagination. Oxford, 1967.

MNC   Map, Walter. *De Nugis Curalium.* Ed. Montague R. James. Oxford, 1914.

GM   Maréchal. See *Guillaume.*

R57   *Margan, Annals of.* In part I of *Annales monastici.* Ed. H. R. Luard. R36, I. London, 1884.

GM   Marshal. See *Guillaume.*

R57   *Matthaei Parisiensis, Monachi Sancti Albani, Chronica Majora.* Ed. H. R. Luard. Seven parts, R57. London, 1872–1884.

MA   *La Mort le roi Artu.* Ed. Jean Frappier, Paris, 1936 also, Geneva (*Textes littéraires français* edition), 1954. References are to section numbers common to both editions, and to line numbers as found in the 1954 edition.

MAS   *Morte Arthur, a romance in stanzas of eight lines.* Ed. J. Douglas Bruce. Early English Text Society, Vol. 88. London, 1903. (Extra Series.)

Vin   *Morte Darthur* of Malory, see Malory.

R82   Newburgh. See William.

RN   Niger. See Ralph.

N   Norgate, Kate. *England under the Angevin Kings.* London, 1887.

NJ   Norgate, Kate. *John Lackland.* London, 1902.

NH   Norgate, Kate. *The Minority of Henry III.* London, 1912.

P   *Patent Rolls, Calendar of the,* Vols. I and V. Public Record Office, London, 1901 and 1910.

Pa   Pauphilet, A. *Le Legs du moyen-âge.* Melun, 1950.

Q   Pauphilet, A. See *Queste.*

PE   Pernoud, Régine. *Eleanor of Aquitaine.* Trans. Peter Wiles. London, 1967.

PB   Peter of Blois. *Opera omnia.* In *Patrologia latina.* Ed. J. P. Migne. Vol. 207, Paris, 1904.

Pic   Picard, Louis Auguste. *Légendes et Miracles de Fontevrault.* Saumur, 1913.

PPR   *Pipe Roll, 17 John, and Praestita Roll, 14–18 John.* Ed. R. A. Brown and J. C. Holt. London, pub. of Pipe Roll Society, N.S. 37 for 1961, issued 1964.

     Pseudo–Map Cycle. see Sommer.

Q   *La Queste del saint Graal.* Ed. A. Pauphilet. Paris, 1923.

R66   Ralph of Coggeshall, *Chronicon Anglicanum.* Ed. Joseph Stevenson. R66, London, 1875. See Rolls.

R68   Ralph of Diceto, *Opera Historica.* Ed. Wm. Stubbs. R68, London, 1876. See Rolls.

RN   Ralph Niger, *Chronica.* Ed. Robert Anstruther. Caxton Society, London, 1851 [rpt. 1967].

     Recueil des Historiens des Gaules et de la France. See *Historiens.*

R99   *Red Book of the Exchequer.* Ed. Hubert Hall. R99, London, 1896. See Rolls.

R82   Richard of Devizes, *Chronicle.* In Part III of *Chronicles of the Reigns of Stephen, Henry II, and Richard I.* Ed. Richard Howlett. R82, III, London, 1888. See Rolls.

Ri   Richardson, H. G., "Letters and Charters of Eleanor of Aquitaine." *English Historical Review,* LXXIV (1959), 193–213.

DP   Roach, Wm. See *Didot-Perceval.*

R82   Robert of Torigni, *Chronicle.* In Part IV of *Chronicles of the Reigns of Stephen, Henry II, and Richard I.* Ed. Richard Howlett. R82, IV, London, 1890. See Rolls.

R51   Roger of Hovedon, *Chronica.* Ed. Wm. Stubbs. Four parts, R51, London, 1868–1871. See Rolls.

R84   Roger of Wendover, *Chronica sive Flores Historiarum.* Ed. H. G. Hewlett. Three parts, R84, London, 1886–1889. See Rolls.

     Rolls. See *Close, Curia Regis, Fine, Inquisitions, Liberate, Patent, Pipe,* and Rolls Series.

R   Rolls Series: *Chronicles and Memorials of Great Britain and Ireland,* Published under the direction of the Master of the

Rolls, 99 volumes. London, 1858–1896. References to all works of the Rolls Series are by R plus arabic numerals representing the volume within the series, plus, if the volume is bound in more than one part, a roman numeral appears to indicate the part. For further description see under the names of the authors or names of the works if the author is unknown or not certainly known:

R38	*Gesta Ricardi, Itinerarium et*	R99	*Red Book of the Exchequer*
R49	*Gesta Henrici*	R82	III Richard of Devizes
R21	Giraldus Cambrensis	R82	IV Robert of Torigni
R37	*Magna Vita Hugonis*	R51	Roger of Hovedon
R36	*Margan Annals*	R84	Roger of Wendover
R57	*Matthew Paris*	R27	*Royal Letters*
R66	Ralph of Coggeshall	R82	I, II, William of
R68	Ralph of Diceto		Newburgh

R27 — *Royal and other historical letters of the reign of Henry III.* Ed. W. W. Shirley. Two parts, R27, London, 1862–1866. See Rolls.

Sa — Salzman, Louis Francis, *Henry II*, Boston, 1914.

Sommer, H. Oskar, ed. *The Vulgate Version of the Arthurian Romances.* Seven volumes plus Index, The Carnegie Institution, Washington, 1908–1916. The Roman numeral shows the volume, the arabic numerals page and line.

St — Stewart, George R. "English Geography in Malory's *Morte Arthure*," *Modern Language Review*, XXX (1935), 204–09.

Su — *Surrey, the Victoria History of the County of.* Ed. H. E. Malden. Vol. III, London, 1911. The section on Guildford is by Dorothy W. Sprites.

R82 — Torigni. See Robert.

SU, WH — Victoria County Histories, see under Surrey and Wiltshire.

Vin — Vinaver, Eugene. See Malory.

Vulgate Cycle. See Sommer.

W — Wace, *Le Roman de Brut de Wace.* Ed. Ivor Arnold. SATF, Paris, 1938–1940.

GM — William Marshal. See *Guillaume.*

R82 — William of Newburgh, *Historia Rerum Anglicarum.* Ed. Richard Howlett. In Parts I and II of the *Chronicles of the Reigns of Stephen, Henry II, and Richard I.* R82 I, II, London 1884. See Rolls.

WH   *Wiltshire, The Victoria History of the County of.* Ed. R. B. Pugh and Elizabeth Crittal, also authors of the section on Amesbury. Vols. III and V, Oxford, 1956–1957.

Wi   "Winchcombe Annals." Ed. R. R. Darlington. In *A Medieval Miscellany for Doris Mary Stenton.* Publication of the Pipe Roll Society, N.S. 36, London, for 1960, issued 1962.

ZRP   See Freymond.

Index

Asterisks (*) precede references to authors and works which are identified only by matter in parentheses at the passages indicated.

147